CHURCHILL
MORTGAGE

Call for a

No Obligation

Consultation

TANE CABE
NMLS ID: 78590; Company NMLS ID: 1591
(www.nmlsconsumeraccess.org)
Branch ID: 99312

Branch Manager   800.490.4287

8805 N. Harborview Dr., Suite 204
Gig Harbor, WA 98332

tane.cabe@churchillmortgage.com

Double
YOUR RETIREMENT
Dollars

Double
YOUR RETIREMENT
Dollars

Little Known Strategies to Quickly Increase Income,
Assets and Cash for Today's Retiree

Tane Cabe

Double Your Retirement Dollars

2nd edition

Cover and Interior Design Indigo Design, Inc

www.bookcoverdesignbyindigo.com

ISBN 978-0-9855500-1-1

Printed in the U.S.A

Contents

PART ONE

Using Your Home Equity as an Asset to Create Income and Buy Real Estate with No Monthly Payment

CHAPTER 3:

We Rarely Get To See Our Children and Grandchildren **33**

CHAPTER 4:

Selling & Buying in a Down Market
(With No Monthly Payment) **39**

CHAPTER 5:

Buy a Home with No Monthly Payment WITHOUT Paying All Cash..............................**45**

CHAPTER 6:

I Don't Qualify for a New Home Purchase Because of My Poor Credit,
Income, and Lack of Down Payment **55**

PART TWO

Using Equity Management to Increase Income, Social Security Benefits, and Estate Planning

"Many do with opportunity as children do at the sea-shore; they fill their little hands with sand, then let the grains fall through one by one, till they are all gone."

– The Royal Path of Life (1876).

Don't let the opportunity contained in this book be like sand through your hands.

Grab hold of the concepts and take action.

Special Note to the Reader

Just like no two stars in the galaxy are alike, no two individuals' retirement situations are exactly the same. The time of writing this book and the time that you hold it in your hand are different – perhaps slightly or dramatically – but different just the same. The information provided at the time of writing may not be exactly the same rules, regulations, and situations today. It's important for you to seek a financial advisor and real estate professional who are knowledgeable in the strategies discussed and that have the most up to date information at their disposal. It's also important that the professional you work with be able to point out the benefits and potential issues with a specific strategy based on your own individual needs and goals. The main objective of this book is to introduce you to powerful concepts and strategies using home equity conversion, real estate, life insurance, and long term care to enhance your retirement through better cash flow and overall planning. This manuscript is not intended to give you any investment or tax advice. Finally, I truly expect you to have some epiphanies from the information contained within and when you do please don't keep this book or its contents a secret!

Introduction

America's 78 million Baby Boomers comprise the largest chunk of the nation's population and carry most of its wealth. Most have paid off their homes and want to age in place. Baby Boomers also have longer life expectancies than previous generations. In fact, according to the American Medical Association, those individuals who make it to age 65 in today's world have a 50 percent chance of living another 25 years.

As you'll read in this book, those extended life spans can be both a blessing and a challenge. After all, it takes money to live and getting old is just darned expensive. There are medical and prescription bills to pay, long-term care worries to think about, and a myriad other expenses that can quickly eat away at your retirement nest egg. And speaking of nest eggs...Baby Boomers aren't exactly prepared for retirement. Between their propensities to spend rather than save – and the recent stock market turmoil and real estate knockdown – many of these individuals have been left wondering just how they're going to afford their Golden Years.

In 1994 Bill Bengen, a financial planner based in Southern California, said retirees should withdraw four percent of their nest egg during their first year of retirement and then increase that dollar amount by the inflation rate every year. If they did this, their savings would easily last them 30 years. He assumed that their portfolio was held in tax-deferred accounts and was split between large company stocks and treasury bonds – very safe investments. In a subsequent study Bengen added other asset mixes, like small companies. Those additions increased portfolio volatility and potential return. To adjust for these factors, Bengen revised the withdrawal rule from four percent to four and a half percent.

But as stocks became more volatile and as people assumed his rule still held true, Bengen was forced to rethink his advice. He now says that the next five years could be crucial for individuals who retire and have experienced major stock market downturns since 2000. He expects the future return on stocks to be low for a while. Coupled with high inflation rates, that will put retirees in tight spots. Many are starting to pull out more than four and a half percent in a volatile market because inflation on those core goods is so high. If this continues, Baby Boomers will run out of money and not know what to do about it.

Bengen sees Home Equity Conversion Mortgages (HECMs) as one viable solution for retirees who want to convert a portion of their home equity into cash. Because of some changes in HECMs (you'll read about them in Chapter Two), many financial advisors now embrace HECMs due to their no-load or low-cost status. They no longer see home equity as the "sacred untouchable cow," and are advising their clients to tap into the largest asset that they have: their homes. And even though real estate values have dropped dramatically, seniors still hold trillions of dollars in home equity. In fact, 65 percent of individuals aged 65 and older own their homes free and clear, according to the U.S. Administration on Aging. That's an awful lot of equity to be sitting on.

That's where the Home Equity Conversion Mortgage comes in. As you'll learn from this book, this innovative financing tool can help senior homeowners tap the wealth that they are literally *sitting* on. While the common approach to homeownership is to buy a home, build equity, and then sell it, I'm here to tell you that there's another, better way to *keep* your home while *tapping* into the huge asset that it is (homeownership is the biggest financial transaction that most people make during their lifetimes, after all).

If you're intrigued, I'd like you to go one step further by answering these questions:

— Do I have enough money to meet my current lifestyle needs?

— Do I have enough money to meet my future lifestyle needs?

— Do I have enough resources to spend time with my family, grandchildren, and friends?

— Am I concerned about my long-term care needs?

— Am I, or is someone I know, retired and in need of additional monthly income?

— Am I concerned about running out of money before I leave this earth?

— Can I afford to do the things that I really want to do during retirement?

— Is my portfolio down?

— Have my assets been reduced to a fearful level?

— Would I like to live in a newer home?

— Would I like to have a second home in a warmer climate?

— Would I like to be able to help my children, grandchildren, or others financially?

— Do I want to leave a financial legacy for my family, church, or others?

If you answered "yes" to one of more of these questions – or if you represent or know someone who would answer yes to them – then you picked up the right book. Maybe you are a consumer who wants to double your retirement dollars, or perhaps you are a financial advisor, insurance professional, elder law attorney, or real estate agent who works with clients who need help. Maybe you have a loved one who is having financial difficulties or problems obtaining long-term care insurance. Whatever your motivating force is, you've come to the right place.

Before I give you an overview of the book's content and how it can work for you, I'd like you to set aside any preconceived notions that you have about money and assets, particularly real estate equity. As you'll learn in Chapter One, (and throughout this book) there are some amazing things you can do when you put home equity to work, what you've read, listened to, or been told about equity and various financial tools is most likely inaccurate, or out of date. As you read through the chapters, keep an open mind, absorb the information, and then internalize it in a way that allows you to make your own decisions about HECMs. Take in all of the information, sample and test it (like you would while standing at a restaurant buffet), and make your own judgments.

Right about now you may be wondering who I am and why I chose to write this book. I've been in the financial and mortgage industries since 1993 and along the way have developed and sold multiple companies. One of them was a software firm that became part of Microsoft's Home Advisor. I've also taught, coached, instructed, and served as a speaker for various financial and mortgage industry panels. For the last eight years I've put a lot of time into studying the plight of seniors and Baby Boomers, looking specifically at how they plan (or don't plan) for retirement. I've worked with many retirees through my own practice and during my teaching and training.

My passion for the subject matter in this book is also personal. I see my own parents working their tails off when they should be retired. They didn't plan for retirement and as a result, must continue working well past the point where they should be enjoying retirement. This is just one aspect of my personal life that drives my passion for helping seniors understand the value that they have in their homes and how they can thrive during retirement (I'm also a card-carrying member of the sandwich generation, but we'll save that for another book!).

The book you're reading is broken up into two sections. The first half deals with real estate – purchasing it, using the equity built up in it, and leveraging it to your advantage. Over 40 percent of people over the age of 60 are planning to move at least once during retirement, according to Fidelity Research Institute, yet most of these people are unaware of HECMs and the value that these financial tools provide. The other 60 percent of people know even less about HECMs. In fact, if the majority did understand the strategies laid out this book, I believe the percentage of "movers" would be much higher.

What's holding these folks back? Income restrictions, credit issues, and the basic fact that we've been taught to build,

build, and build our home equity from the time we buy a home until we pass away. Moving during retirement – even if it means being closer to grandchildren or the seashore – isn't in the typical person's plans. And even if the family home is way too large and difficult for a senior to maintain, that steadfast stance remains the driving force behind staying put.

The second section of the book addresses financial planning issues, takes into consideration your "holistic" financial picture, and shows you how to create additional income on a monthly basis. I'll give you strategies to increase your Social Security, transfer wealth, take care of your long-term care needs, and create income using your current assets. You'll learn how to retire at 62 and still preserve your Social Security benefits. You'll also learn how to not take IRA distributions and still retire in style.

This book is designed to be read from cover to cover, but don't be afraid to give it an initial thumb-through. Read the chapter headings, skim through the sections, and then go back and identify the specific areas that relate to your individual situation. Even after you've completed your first HECM you'll want to refer to this book regularly for new ideas and thoughts on how to leverage this excellent financial tool in other ways.

If you're ready to get started on your journey, just flip on over to Part One.

PART ONE

Using Your Home Equity
as an Asset to Create Income
and Buy Real Estate
with No Monthly Payment

CHAPTER 1

The Financial Challenges of Retiring

The nation's Baby Boomers are woefully unprepared for retirement. Saddled with debt, still reeling from the recent recession and stock market plunge, and working well past their intended retirement ages, the group of individuals born between 1946 and 1964 need help. Although more than half of retirees aged 65 and older (64 percent of total retirees) get at least half of their retirement income from Social Security, there is also a significant portion of the population of retirees whose primary source of retirement income is a portfolio of securities, often in a pre-tax account such as a 401(k) plan or a rollover individual retirement account (IRA).[1]

Most retirees are afraid of running out of money before they run out of time. They fear outliving their financial resources and, unfortunately, with all of the government challenges and political pressures on Social Security and the nation's health care system, the odds that this fear will become a reality are very high. The scenario isn't expected to improve anytime soon. Obamacare, talk of Social Security reserves running out, and other news in the media point to a future where retirees

---

1 Brandon, Emily, How to Retire on Social Security Alone, U.S. News & World Report (May 16, 2011).

who chose to ignore the inevitable and who *don't* explore alternative financial sources will find themselves in dire straits.

It's Time for a Change

For many Baby Boomers, the issues creating the greatest negative impact on their retirement portfolios are well out of their control. Sure they may not have saved enough during their early years, but add the world's geopolitical problems and inflation to the mix and you literally wind up with a recipe for disaster. As America's world power status continues to wane, and as its currency loses ground against other international options, inflation begins to take hold and chips away at consumer spending power. Leading-edge Baby Boomers (born between 1946 and 1955) are particularly fearful of this situation (even if some of the information is being fed to them through sensationalistic news channels).

The good news is that there is hope, and it's literally staring you in the face right now. In this book, you're going to learn about an effective tool that other Americans are already using to balance out the equation and get a handle on their retirement plans. You're going to learn about how Robert, an 83-year-old single man, sold the $600,000 waterfront property that was bleeding him dry due to high mortgage payments. A retired teacher, Robert used the proceeds of the sale to pay off his mortgage and the balance to purchase a brand new $418,000 home with no mortgage payments. He used a down payment of $187,000 to buy his new home, supplemented his retirement income with an additional $203,000 in cash, and never had another mortgage payment for the rest of his life.

When I asked Robert what he planned on doing with the $200,000+ in proceeds that he pocketed from the sale, he said, "I just wanted to party." He wanted to have fun. He moved into the city to get closer to the "fun" and to the medical facilities and other necessities that help him live an enjoyable, healthy life during his golden years.

As you read through this book you'll also hear about how Sheryl and Randy purchased a home for $480,000. They put less than 50 percent down on that home and never will have another mortgage payment as long as they live in that house. Another individual – a single, 62-year-old woman – purchased a home for $299,000 with $140,000 down and freed herself up from monthly mortgage payments. She can't stop talking about how much she enjoys living in her new home and how awesome it is to <u>not</u> have a mortgage payment. She tells everyone she can about the HECM and how it completely changed her life and financial status.

John and Elizabeth made a similar move, but actually decided to stay in their existing home since they owned it free and clear. Using a HECM, they opened a line of credit (you'll learn more about this strategy later in this book) and virtually ensured that they will never run out of retirement funds. That's because the line of credit that they're using will continue to grow. Fifteen years from now they'll have several hundred thousand dollars that they'll be able to access with no monthly payment obligations whatsoever (as long as they continue to reside in their home). It's an extra bucket of money that they were able to create out of thin air thanks to the significant amount of equity that that couple has in the home.

Creating New Revenue Streams

Homeowners are also using HECMs to create additional income for themselves. Both in their early-70s, John and Sarah bring in about $2,000 a month in Social Security and pension income and pay out $1,700 of that in monthly mortgage payments. They were literally scraping to get by and sitting on a $180,000 home mortgage. What they *did* have was enough equity in their home to use a HECM to pay off their mortgage (completely wiping out that $1,700 a month payment) and live off of that $2,000 per month without having to worry about how to afford groceries and unexpected expenses.

HECMs are also a valuable tool for multifamily homebuyers. Don, 65, recently purchased a $300,000 duplex and then rented out the other side of his home to a tenant for $850 per month. He put $148,000 down on the duplex and now has no monthly mortgage payment *plus* a positive income stream of $850 a month. This is just one simple example of how a HECM can help you generate income and offset the financial challenges presented by retirement.

In this book you'll also hear the stories of couples and individuals who have gone beyond the financial advantages of using a HECM to create real and meaningful lifestyle changes for themselves. When 70-year-old Eric retired, for example, he and his wife Susan (aged 65) were making very large monthly payments on their $480,000 mortgage. Susan continued working to support that obligation, but the couple also had a lot of equity in their home. After selling the property, they put $187,000 down on a smaller, more management home – a move that allowed Susan to retire. They also came away with an extra $100,000 in cash proceeds from the sale of their home (after down payment and closing costs on the new property).

Eric and Susan are now both retired from work and enjoying a new, simpler lifestyle.

Tapping the Power of the HECM

As you can see, there are many different financial scenarios and lifestyle challenges that can be addressed by a Home Equity Conversion Mortgage. Unfortunately, the HECM is a valuable solution that *very few people know about.* With this book as your guide, you'll be able to successfully navigate the HECM waters and achieve financial dreams and goals that you thought were completely unattainable.

Four Things to Remember from Chapter One:

1. The nation's Baby Boomers are woefully unprepared for retirement.

1. Most retirees are afraid of running out of money before they run out of time.

1. In this book you'll also hear the stories of couples and individuals who have gone beyond the financial advantages of using a HECM to create real and meaningful lifestyle changes for themselves.

1. There are many different financial scenarios and lifestyle challenges that can be addressed by a Home Equity Conversion Mortgage.

CHAPTER 2

Objections You Have – The Truth About Home Equity Conversion Mortgages

HECMs are extremely useful financial tools that tend to get a bad rap from those who don't understand them or don't have up-to-date information or focus on media sound bites that fall woefully short of fully factual treatment of the subject. In reality, HECMs provide a viable route for older homeowners to cash-out, transfer wealth to younger family members, pay off loans, catch up on bills, maximize their Social Security benefits, and make a myriad of other positive financial moves.

As with all fiction there is usually some element of fact. HECM objections and fears are based partly on fact. The number one objection that is based on historical fact but *not true today* is that the lender will take the borrowers home. I still hear people say, "I guess I am ready to give my house to the bank so I can get a HECM." The earlier HECM programs prior to government involvement and regulation did take the title to the home and borrowers gave up their rights to ownership. Unfortunately, people still believe this to be the case, however HECM lenders do not take the title and don't want your home. Your title is safe and you don't give your house to the lender when obtaining a HECM.

A HECM is just the opposite of a traditional mortgage. With a traditional mortgage the borrower must pay the lender minimum monthly scheduled payments or more until the balance is paid in full. Once the loan is paid in full the home is considered to be owned free and clear of any mortgage. A HECM is just the opposite. The borrower does not have to pay a monthly scheduled payment but rather the HECM pays them. The payment received (or cash proceeds) is paid from the equity in the home. The balance on the HECM grows as interest on the loan accrues and proceeds are used. As the balance grows it uses more and more equity. Every year the balance on the HECM grows compared to a traditional mortgage where the balance decreases.

Just so we are clear, even though you don't pay a monthly payment out of your pocket, the interest charged on a HECM is paid by using the equity stored in the home. For example, if a borrower has a home valued at $250,000 with an original HECM balance of $160,000, he may have a balance of $210,000 by year five. The equity used to pay for interest in the five-year period was $50,000. This option may not settle well with some, but rest assured the borrower will never owe more than the house is worth. Not having a mortgage payment, but receiving cash each month or in a lump sum can mean all the difference especially in retirement.

Some of the confusion over HECMs stems from the fact that not everyone understands them or how they work. From a fairly young age Americans are taught that the dream of owning a home is facilitated by taking out a first mortgage from a lender and then paying off that loan.

For many people, the buck stops there. If it's not sold before the loan term ends the home is then paid off and retained until it's time to transfer it to one or more heirs. What many homeowners don't realize is that there is an easy way to turn their castles into cash using a HECM. This tax-exempt home loan allows individuals aged 62 or older to use their home equity to "cash out" without having to sell their properties and without taking on the burden of additional monthly payments.

The Nuts and Bolts of HECMs

There are a few important parameters for HECMs, including:

— At least one of the homeowners must be 62 or older.

— He or she must occupy the property as a principal residence.

— Properties that qualify for HECMs include:

— Single-family residences

— Condominiums

— Townhouses

— Manufactured homes built after June 1976.

— Interest from a HECM is tax deductible, but not until the loan is paid off in part or in full.

Once you move out of your home, you must pay back the loan plus interest and any other fees to the mortgage lender, but the remaining equity will be yours, and *the debt can never exceed the value of your home.*

— The terms on HECMs vary and include both fixed and variable rate options.

— The homeowner pays the loan origination fees, servicing fees, and any other closing costs for the HECM.

— HECMs are non-recourse loans. A non-recourse loan is

where the borrower is not personally liable for the debt. When compared to a full-recourse loan the borrower is fully liable in addition to the collateralized property.

There are three types of HECMs: single-purpose; federally insured; and proprietary. There are variations among these three options but the basic premise of the HECM remains the same across all of them. Here's a description of each option to help you discern among them:

1. **Single-purpose:** These HECMs are typically offered to lower-income homeowners who obtain the loans through non-profit organizations and government agencies. In most cases the loans are used to pay off property taxes or to make home improvements that the owner wouldn't otherwise be able to afford. The fees associated with single-purpose HECMs are low, but the programs are limited in terms of what the cash can be used for.

2. **Federally insured:** Also known as Home Equity Conversion Mortgages (HECM), these are less restrictive than the single-purpose HECMs but typically are associated with higher costs (fees, closing costs, and so forth). The U.S. Department of Housing and Urban Development (HUD) backs federally-insured HECMs and requires homeowners to meet with independent, government-approved housing counselors before closing on any such loans. These HECMs come with a great deal of flexibility; homeowners can select how they want to receive and spend the money. HECMs carry the same interest rates (regardless of the individual lender) but servicing fees and closing costs may vary.

3. **Proprietary:** The proprietary HECM comes with flexibility in terms of how the money is distributed (a line of credit, monthly installments, etc.). These mortgages tend to be more expensive than HECMs because private lenders back the loans. Homeowners who use this strategy can obtain more money upfront (than a HECM), but the initial credit line will not grow over time.

The federally-insured HECM is the most popular choice for HECMs because it offers the most flexibility and is applicable for the largest cross section of homeowners aged 62 and older.

How HECMs Work

HECMs work the opposite of traditional home mortgages by allowing owners who have accumulated home equity to pull cash out of their investments using monthly installments, a lump sum payment, or a line of credit. Unless otherwise specified by the lender, the funds can be used to pay for a wide range of expenses.

As you'll read throughout this book, everyone from the grandmother who wants to fund her grandson's college education to the retiree who wants to buy a second home in Florida to the 62+ homeowner who doesn't qualify for a new home purchase can benefit from a HECM. What makes this financial instrument particularly attractive is the fact that it *doesn't* result in a new monthly payment for the homeowner.

In most cases the HECM doesn't have to be repaid because over time it depletes the home's equity. Here are a few exceptions to that rule:

— The owner fails to pay property taxes.

— The owner fails to pay homeowners insurance.

— The owner allows the property to deteriorate and fall into disrepair.

— The owner moves to a new principal residence.

— The owner lives elsewhere for 12 successive months.

If any of the above occurs, then the owner will have to pay off the HECM balance plus any associated fees or interest.

Breaking Down the Barriers

HECMs garner support from backers who range from individual homeowners to lenders to national groups like the American Association of Retired Persons (AARP), which has issued recommendations in favor of HECMs. In fact, the consumer advocate organization says HECMs "can be tremendously positive for borrowers" who fully understand how these vehicles work.

Would the AARP *really* speak in favor of a financial tool that *wasn't* beneficial for such a high percentage of individuals aged 62 and over? I didn't think so either. Still, a number of myths and rumors continue to circulate around the industry. Here are just a few of the *untruths* you may have encountered:

1. **The Lender Will Take the Home Out from Under the Homeowner.** The idea that signing on the dotted line for a HECM is tantamount to giving a home away is the single biggest myth that keeps owners from enjoying the financial benefits of this vehicle. The idea that the lender will somehow take the home out from under the owner is simply a myth. In fact, the borrower retains perpetual ownership of the home

and is able to enjoy the value of that home (through cash payments, a line of credit, or other distribution choice) while he or she is living. The HECM's role is to guarantee that the lender will be repaid for any remaining loan amount. To make sure this happens, HECM borrowers pay a mandatory 2 percent insurance fee to the government, which in turn assures the repayment. Private lenders guarantee the other types of HECMs.

2. **The Property Must be Paid Off and/or Debt-Free for the Owner to Qualify.** Not true. In fact, HECMs were created to help owners convert their home equity into cash. While there must be sufficient equity in the home, the original mortgage (or, any seconds or thirds on the property) needn't be paid off for a home to be eligible. In many instances owners use HECMs to pay off existing home loans, thus eliminating the need for any monthly payments (since the HECM doesn't come with any new monthly payments).

3. **Lenders Put the Property Up for Sale When the Mortgage is Due.** Quite the contrary. The owner controls his or her home and retains the title. An heir may sell the property in order to repay the loan, but the lender itself doesn't have that kind of control. In most cases, the heirs of senior homeowners appreciate the fact that their parents or grandparents have a financial tool that allows them to reside in their own homes in an independent, financially secure fashion.

4. **When the Owner Dies, the Lender Gets the House.** When the owner passes away the HECM follows the same procedure as a traditional mortgage, with

the home transferring to either the estate or to the borrower's heirs. The borrower's passing will trigger the HECM to be due and payable. The estate or heirs can sell the home, pay the balance with cash, or refinance it with a traditional mortgage to satisfy the debt. Regardless of the market value of the home the only obligation to the estate is the loan balance. If the home is worth less than the HECM balance the estate is not responsible for the difference. The mortgage insurance will pay any shortage between the value of the home and the balance on the HECM.

5. **The Homeowner Could Wind Up "Upside Down" Financially.** This can't happen. In fact, a homeowner can't ever owe more than the home's value on a HECM. Additionally, HECMs are insured by the FHA, making them that much more secure for homeowners who are 62+ and looking for ways to free up the equity in their homes.

6. **The Lender Will Dictate How the Money is Used.** How the money is spent is left up to the borrower in most cases. Debts, loans, travel expenses, or even that second home in Florida can be financed with the proceeds generated by a HECM.

7. **HECMs are Expensive.** This statement is based on historical fact but now is untrue. Historically the standard HECM closing fees were high when compared with traditional conventional mortgages. A typical HECM on a $250,000 home could come with a hefty closing cost structure, often $15,000 or more. The costs were high due to the standard 2 percent origination fees and mortgage insurance premiums.

When compared to a conventional mortgage the same $250,000 home could have closing costs of $6,000 or less. However, if you take less money out up front while lowering your total obligations, then your mortgage insurance will be just 0.5 percent (rather than 2.5 percent). If you own your home free and clear, your total obligations would be lower.

Additionally, only HUD allowed fees are permitted, and no markups or junk fees can be tagged onto the loans. Typical there are also no out-of-pocket costs for the loan (most are incorporated into the loan balance) with the exception of the property appraisal cost (typically $350-$600, depending on geographic location).

8. **The Transaction will Generate a Hefty Tax Bill.**
Nope. In fact, unlike most investment proceeds, the cash distributed from a HECM transaction does not generate any type of taxable event. The funds are classified as a loan on equity in the home and are never taxable. Borrowers are responsible for property taxes and insurance, any association dues, maintaining the property, and abiding by the terms of the loan.

9. **HECMs are Only for the "Cash Poor" Homeowners.**
Nothing could be further from the truth. HECMs are excellent financial planning tools that homeowners across all socioeconomic levels can benefit from. Seniors who own multimillion-dollar homes, for example, frequently use HECMs as part of their estate plans, knowing that the option can help facilitate the greatest transfer of wealth to the next generation.

10. **The Owner Will Need Good Credit to Qualify for a HECM.** Unlike the traditional mortgage, the HECM requires no income checks or credit score requirements to qualify. This gives homeowners a big advantage during the transaction since they don't have to prove creditworthiness or income to get the HECM. The lender simply looks at the home itself, its condition, and the homeowner's equity when making the decision. Other considerations include taxes and any other government debts that may be outstanding (see the first section of this chapter for the requirements associated with HECMs).

11. **Social Security, Medicare and Other Benefits Will Be Adversely Affected by the HECM.** This final myth keeps a high number of seniors from realizing the benefits of a HECM. Afraid of losing their benefits they instead suffer on a check-to-check basis, never knowing that the equity they are sitting on could be making their lives a lot easier. Social Security and Medicare are not affected because the HECM is a loan and it's not considered income. Medicaid is not affected either.

There are many other myths swirling around the HECM industry, which over the last decade has matured into a reliable, valuable part of any senior's investment portfolio. Whether they are well off financially or in need of an economic boost, any homeowner aged 62 or older would be wise to investigate their options in this realm.

Key Questions Answered

HUD provides oversight of the HECM industry and FHA's HECM program. "The HECM is a safe plan that can give older Americans greater financial security," states the HUD website. "Many seniors use it to supplement Social Security, meet unexpected medical expenses, make home improvements, and more." Here, the government organization addresses the key queries that consumers typically have regarding HECMs:

1. **Can I qualify for FHA's HECM?**

   To be eligible for a FHA HECM, the FHA requires that you or any other borrower be a homeowner 62 years of age or older, own your home outright or have a low mortgage balance (generally 50 percent equity or more) that can be paid off at closing with proceeds from the reverse loan, and you must live in the home. You are also required to receive consumer information free or at very low cost from a HECM counselor prior to obtaining the loan. (You can find a HECM counselor online or by phoning (800) 569-4287.)

2. **Can I apply if I didn't buy my present house with an FHA-insured mortgage?**

   Yes. It doesn't matter if you didn't buy it with an FHA-insured mortgage. Your new FHA HECM will be FHA-insured.

3. **What types of homes are eligible?**

   To be eligible for the FHA HECM, your home must be a single family home or a 1-4 unit home with one unit occupied by the borrower. HUD-approved condominiums and manufactured homes that meet FHA requirements are also eligible.

4. What's the difference between a HECM and a bank home equity loan?

With a traditional second mortgage or a home equity line of credit, you must have a sufficient income versus debt ratio to qualify for the loan, and you are required to make monthly mortgage payments. The HECM is different in that it pays you and is available regardless of your current income. The amount you can borrow depends on your age, the current interest rate, and the appraised value of your home, sales price, or FHA's mortgage limits – whichever is less. Generally, the more valuable your home is, the older you are, and the lower the interest rate, the more you may borrow.

With a HECM, you don't make monthly principal and interest payments, the lender pays you according to the payment plan you select. Like all homeowners, you still are required to pay your real estate taxes, insurance, and other conventional payments like utilities. With an FHA HECM you cannot be foreclosed or forced to vacate your house because you "missed your mortgage payment."

5. Will I still have an estate that I can leave to my heirs?

When you sell your home, you or your estate will repay the cash you received from the HECM plus interest and other fees, to the lender. The remaining equity in your home, if any, belongs to you or to your heirs.

6. How much money can I get from my home?

The amount you can borrow depends on:

a. Age of the youngest borrower

b. Current interest rate

c. Lesser of the appraised value of your home, the HECM FHA mortgage limit for your area, or the sales price

d. The initial Mortgage Insurance Premium (MIP) would either be 2.5 percent (this would be the upfront premium). 2.5 percent if your maximum obligations are maximized, and then 0.5 percent if your total obligations are less than 60 percent.

You can borrow more with the HECM Standard option. If there is more than one borrower, the age of the youngest borrower is used to determine the amount you can borrow.

7. **Should I use an estate planning service to find a HECM?**

FHA does NOT recommend using any service that charges a fee for referring a borrower to an FHA lender. FHA provides this information free, and HECM housing counselors are available for free or at a very low cost, to provide information, counseling, and a free referral to a list of FHA-approved lenders.

8. **What if I am over 62 and my spouse is not?**

In August 2014 the FHA allowed borrowers to include a spouse who is younger than 62. The FHA will release new principal limit factors (or lower loan amount calculations) based on the younger borrower's age. Since that has not been the case historically, we are using principal limit factors that are based on the youngest borrower with a minimum age of 62. For example, if the borrowers are 65 and 55, we are using new calculations or new limit factors that will include the younger spouse. The loan amount calculations will be based on the younger spouse's age. Keep in mind that at least one spouse must be 62 or older.

9. **How do I receive my payments?**
   You have five options:

   a. **Tenure** - Equal monthly payments as long as at least one borrower lives and continues to occupy the property as a principal residence.

   b. **Term** - Equal monthly payments for a fixed period of months selected.

   c. **Line of Credit** - Unscheduled payments or installments, at times and in amounts of your choosing until the line of credit is exhausted.

   d. **Modified Tenure** - Combination of line of credit with monthly payments for as long as you remain in the home.

   e. **Modified Term** - Combination of line of credit plus monthly payments for a fixed period of months selected by the borrower.

Using the information above, and the rest of the myth-busting details outlined in this chapter, you will be well braced to take advantage of HECMs. For unlike those detractors who have tried to give the industry a negative reputation, you now know that this vehicle can serve as a viable tool for a wide variety of senior homeowners.

FHA's Sweeping Changes Shore Up the HECM Program

In late-2013, the FHA made changes that helped ensure the longevity and security of the HECM program. This is a particularly important point because America's seniors and Baby Boomers are afraid of running out of money and are also fearful that the HECM program may be eliminated. The FHA's solution to these worries was to shore up the program and announce that – despite the fact that so many mortgage insurance claims were filed during the housing crisis – the HECM isn't going away anytime soon. Before the changes many HECM borrowers elected to obtain the fixed rate program. The fixed program required the borrower to take all the available proceeds at closing. This presented a problem for people that don't have a mortgage to pay and find themselves with a large lump sum of cash. Since interest on the loan will accumulate on a larger balance it will grow more rapidly.

Let's say Alan owned his $500,000 home free and clear. Using simple math, under the old rules, he'd have to borrow $250,000 using a fixed-rate HECM (with an estimated $250,000 coming at closing). That scenario changed dramatically when the housing market dropped – namely because Alan's $500,000 home was suddenly worth $300,000 (or less, depending on where he lived). With a $250,000 mortgage balance and an interest rate of 5 percent, the latter accumulated at a greater rate on a monthly basis due to the higher loan amount. Alan winds up in a situation where he owes $375,000 on a $300,000 home. When he passes away, the HECM balance is due – yet the value of the home is lower than the actual mortgage balance. FHA is now paying out a high dollar volume in such claims and recently commissioned a study and learned that it was $980 million short due to this situation. That's what caused the organization to put the brakes on things in the HECM realm in October of 2013. They recalculated and recalibrated the program and eliminated the *when people own their home free and clear* clause that forced homeowners to borrow all of those funds. Now, borrowers are limited and people are beginning to use more variable rate products and those that include credit lines (which we'll delve into more deeply later in this book).

Financial Industry Giant Gives Its Stamp of Approval

If the basic truths about HECMs aren't enough to convince you of their value, consider this: In 2008 one of the world's largest insurance firms got into the HECM business. Long known for its tenacity for protecting seniors, MetLife, Inc. (via its subsidiary MetLife Bank) purchased EverBank Reverse Mortgage LLC. The latter has since morphed into an operating subsidiary of MetLife Bank.

In the next chapter we'll look at the first scenario in which a HECM can translate into a myriad of positive impacts for borrowers. Up first: how grandparents can use HECMs to move closer to their families and spend more time with their grandchildren.

Four Things to Remember from Chapter Two:

1. Most of the negative news associated with HECMs is untrue or outdated.

2. Homeowners aged 62 or over can use HECMs in countless ways.

3. A borrower needn't be "cash poor" to use a HECM, which can serve as a valuable investment or estate planning vehicle.

4. Good credit, significant equity, and/or a home that's paid off are not prerequisites for HECM approval.

Take the Quiz! "Is a HECM Right For Me?" Take the quiz by visiting **doubleyourretirementdollars.com/quiz**

To watch a video explanation of HECMs visit **doubleyouretirementdollars.com/reversevideo.com**

CHAPTER 3:

We Rarely Get To See Our Children and Grandchildren

As the 73 million-strong Baby Boomer generation continues to move into its retirement years, and as the generation that came before it enjoys its golden years, an increasing number of Americans will be looking for flexible financing and housing options.

One particularly hot issue for these seniors will be the time spent away from their children and grandchildren who reside in other states. Moving to another city or an entirely different state are the possible solutions to this dilemma, but not all retirees have the funds or credit necessary to afford such a move.

John and Sara Wilson fit into this category. The couple resided in a condominium in Anacortes, Wash., but lamented the fact that they missed out on face time with their children and grandchildren in Northern California. News about little league games, soccer practices, and school recitals has to be shared via phone or over the Internet. Precious moments are missed, holidays are lonely, and electronic communications become a mainstay for keeping the family together.

Solving the Problem

In this case the biggest issue was not the geographical divide, but the fact that limited, fixed incomes kept the parties from seeing one another. Airline tickets, hotel stays, and rental cars are expensive propositions for individuals who are living on tight budgets. Both in their 80s, John and Sara stayed up at night many times, discussing the problem and trying to come up with solutions. They came up empty.

That was, until they learned about HECMs from a real estate professional in their area. Working with him and with a HECM specialist, the Wilsons' eyes were opened to a financial option that they've never considered. It was quite a revelation, and one that this couple will *never* forget!

With the housing market down at the time in Northern California, it seemed like the perfect opportunity to take out a HECM to purchase a home closer to their children. The Wilsons had some cash in certificates of deposit coming due at the bank. The CD's were not creating any income but provided liquidity in case of emergency. They decided to use the cash from the CD's to cover a down payment and closing costs for the home in California, thus allowing the couple to achieve their goals without having to sacrifice themselves financially or take on another monthly bill.

They purchased the home in California for $158,000 using $58,675 in cash reserves from their CDs, the remaining was funded using a HECM on the California home. They rented out their Washington condo – which had been paid off years earlier – for $950 per month which will provide extra income per month and build back up their cash reserves.

Today the Wilsons are free to spend as much time with their children and grandchildren that they want. They can go to soccer games, play with the kids, and lounge around on the playground while the youngsters have fun. John and Sara also created an additional income stream for themselves with the HECM (home equity conversion mortgage), which helped them generate $950 a month in rent.

Rather than being forced to sell their home in a down real estate market, the Wilsons were able to effectively parlay their equity into the cash they needed to create a freer, more enjoyable lifestyle for themselves.

The Wilsons are in good company. All across America today's "mobile" generations are taking jobs and entering into relationships that take them far from their loved ones. Those left behind must scramble to come up with plans that allow them to see their children and grandchildren. Through the HECM process these individuals can be reunited with their families and enjoy the rest of their lives as part of a complete unit.

Let's Do the Math

John and Sara Wilson were perfect candidates for a HECM based on the fact that their primary home was paid off, the market was unfavorable for selling, and they had a true desire to move to another state: to spend time with their family. Here's how they handled their HECM:

They owned their condominium in Anacortes, Washington free and clear.

Age of the youngest borrower:	80
Loan balance on the condo:	Zero
Purchase price of the new home:	$158,000

HECM loan amount on new purchase: $105,070

Down payment and closing costs for new purchase: $59,503

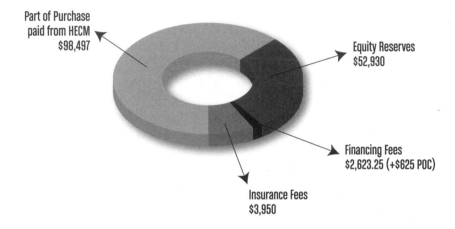

The Wilson's HECM was a godsend for the couple. They'd all but given up trying to figure out how to spend more time with their children and grandchildren without having to sell their Washington condo in a down market. It was a win-win situation for the couple, providing them with $950 in rental income and the ability to purchase a $158,000 home with no monthly payments. Isn't that incredible? What other financial option can you think of that would allow these geographically isolated homeowners to get closer to their families without having to sell their home or tap more retirement reserves? That's right – there are none!

In the next chapter we'll examine an issue that's plaguing many consumers in today's market: how to sell and buy in a down market. You'll learn that even when the market says "no" HECMs can open doors that were previously closed to a wide range of senior homeowners.

Four Things to Remember from Chapter Three:

1. Senior homeowners have an excellent financial tool known as a HECM in their back pockets.

2. HECMs can help older homeowners make major moves that were unthinkable without the help of a HECM.

3. Family comes first for many older homebuyers, but market conditions and long-term homeownership prevent them from exploring their options.

4. The quality of life for aging Americans can be enhanced by a simple mechanism known as a HECM.

CHAPTER 4:

Selling & Buying in a Down Market (With No Monthly Payment)

Every winter a high number of retirees living in the nation's northern climates make their pilgrimage to Florida. They load up their SUVs, minivans, and cars and hop onto I-95 for a direct route to the Sunshine State, where residents refer to these part-time visitors as "snowbirds." Earning that title can take a lifetime for many retirees in states like Michigan, Illinois, New York, and Pennsylvania – where the cold winters only get more unbearable as the aging process kicks in.

Some retirees face major obstacles when it comes time to move south. Real estate markets are down across most of the country and home mortgages aren't being doled out as freely as they once were. Many individuals worry that they'll get buried under a pile of new monthly payments, insurance fees, property tax payments, and repair and maintenance costs associated with their homes. The coveted "snowbird" title can quickly fade out of site, leaving retirees to grapple with the bitter cold and snow in their own backyards.

That's the situation that Mike and Julie Sullivan were facing recently. Long-time residents of Chicago, the Sullivan's owned their home and carried a small balance on their mortgage. The retired couple had enough retirement savings to live comfortably in the windy city, but they had a deep-rooted desire to escape the state's cold winters. They didn't want to sell their home in the down market, but they weren't getting any younger either.

Living in a sunny, warm climate was an extremely attractive proposition that the Sullivan's discussed frequently and with enthusiasm. Doctors even got behind the Sullivan's' dreams of moving south by telling them that the warm weather would help them maneuver better and become more active.

While the arguments for moving were certainly valid, the Sullivans were worried. They'd done a fairly good job of saving for retirement and were receiving regular retirement income. What they didn't want to do was cash out their IRAs to be able to purchase another home in Winter Haven, Fla., where homes range in price from $150,000 to $200,000. Should they decide to move, the Sullivan's wanted to be able to pay cash for the home and not incur a new monthly mortgage payment.

But the lure of the Sunshine State was downright magnetic. The Sullivan's had friends in Chicago who spent their winters as snowbirds in Winter Haven. When those birds flew south for the winter they left the Sullivan's and other friends behind to fend for themselves in Chicago's snow, freezing temps, and frequent blizzards.

The Sullivans were torn. The issue of where to live and how to afford a move kept them up at night and caused tension in their marriage. If they sold their home they'd lose money because of market conditions. They wouldn't walk away with enough cash to purchase an abode in Winter Haven – something they were beginning to see as the Holy Grail. And even though Florida's property values were at very low levels (compared to the early-2000s), the Sullivan's just couldn't piece the puzzle together without excessive worry about money. They were literally frozen in the headlights, not wanting to sell and not wanting to suffer through another winter.

Solving the Problem

The Sullivan's found the answers they were looking for from a HECM specialist who walked them through the purchase process and showed the couple how they could benefit from the financing option. Local real estate agents in both states also played their part in seeing the deal through to fruition.

The Sullivans couldn't believe their ears. Could it possibly be true that using the HECM program they'd be able to list their Chicago home for sale, sell it at a reduced price (for a cash sale), and generate enough money for the $150,000 to $200,000 home in Florida? That would be simply amazing for the winter-weary couple!

And even though the Sullivans would have to say goodbye to their snowbird friends (who fly back up north for the summer) every spring, they know they can make more friends to fill the gap. They know that the social scene is active and the outdoor activities, theme parks, and tourist attractions will keep them busy.

Thanks to the HECM program, the Sullivans were able to purchase a $200,000 home in Winter Haven *without* having to fork over that much cash up front. Their down payment was more than $100,000 and they are living mortgage-free. They also got rid of the monthly mortgage payment on their Chicago home and made their own permanent pilgrimage to the Sunshine State. They sit by the pool year-round (except for the occasional "cold front," when the temps dip below 70 degrees), play golf and cards, go shopping, and have a great time with their friends in Winter Haven.

Had the Sullivans *not* taken advantage of the HECM for purchase program they wouldn't be where they are today. In fact, they'd be either in the middle of one rough winter or preparing for the next one. They were able to put less cash down on their new home and still avoid a mortgage payment. They wound up with cash reserves and added that money to their retirement war chest. It was a great move for them and they couldn't be happier.

So what happened to the Sullivan's Chicago home? They sold it quickly at a price that the market would bear and then used 50 percent of the proceeds for the down payment on their new home. Again, they didn't generate a new monthly mortgage payment and are sitting in an even better financial position than they were just a few months earlier. They're living it up in Florida, getting along great, and loving every minute of it!

Let's Do the Math

Mike and Julie Sullivan were stuck in a winter rut and didn't know what to do about it. They've saved for retirement and were living off the income generated by those efforts, but they really wanted to move to a warmer climate. In fact, their doctors even advised it for health reasons. Here's how they sold their home in a down market and turned their dreams into reality with a new home in Florida:

Sales price for Illinois home:	$310,000
Age of youngest borrower	68
Loan balance on home sold:	$38,690

Loan payment on home sold:	$633.18
Total net proceeds from sale of home:	$246,510
HECM Loan Amount:	$113,800
Mortgage Insurance Premium:	$5,000
Down payment and closing costs (aka shortfall):	$93,991
Total remaining for moving expenses and savings	$152,519
Net positive cash flow (with no more mortgage payment):	**$833.18**

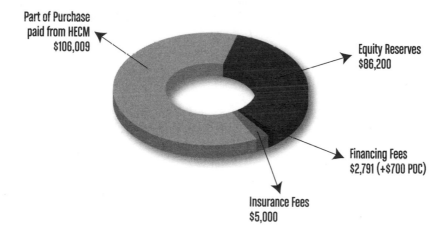

Part of Purchase paid from HECM $106,009

Equity Reserves $86,200

Financing Fees $2,791 (+$700 POC)

Insurance Fees $5,000

The Sullivans now have over $150,000 in extra cash for retirement and have also improved their monthly cash flow by $633.18. Better yet, they live in a warm, sunny climate year-round and are enjoying their healthy, happy retirement years in Florida. Would this have been possible through more traditional financial avenues? Absolutely not. There's no way that this type of win-win deal could have possibly solved the Sullivans' issues while also fulfilling their lifelong dreams.

It's truly unfortunate, but there are a lot of couples like the Sullivans out there who *don't* have an understanding about the value of HECMs for their individual situations. Do you or anyone you know want to get their snowbird dreams launched!

In the next chapter we'll explore the "cash is king" scenario and show how a HECM can help retirees buy their homes outright and without incurring any new monthly housing payments.

Four Things to Remember from Chapter Four:

1. Retiring to a warm climate is a lifelong dream for many, but isn't always attainable through traditional mortgages.

2. The down market has made it difficult for current homeowners to sell their properties and move south.

3. A HECM provides a valuable bridge for eligible homeowners who must sell in a down market.

4. Using a HECM, homeowners can generate cash for down payments and also increase their monthly cash flows by investing the remainder of the proceeds.

CHAPTER 5:

Buy a Home
with No Monthly Payment
WITHOUT Paying All Cash

So far in this book we've looked at situations where HECMs proved their value in helping homeowners get out of negative financial situations and/or life challenges where traditional mortgages would provide little or no value. You've read about grandmothers who helped their children achieve the dream of homeownership, snowbirds who flew south to warmer weather and healthier lives, and seniors who used the HECMs to help them move closer to their children and grandchildren.

Now let's look at how HECMs for purchase can help financially-savvy homeowners who have plenty of resources, but who want to save them for better things rather than down payments and housing payments.

A few years ago there was a married couple that had literally dotted all of the I's and crossed all of the T's when it came to retirement planning. Todd and Joan Wilson were drawing $3,250 a month from Todd's pension (he'd put in over 30 years at a large corporation) and a Social Security income of $1,785 per month. They also had $568,977 in IRA assets. In total, the Wilsons were bringing in about $10,000 a month. Not bad at all in an era where so few Americans have planned appropriately for retirement!

Todd and Joan were obviously financially savvy. They saved money and knew the value of having cash on hand and less tied up in equity, particularly in a market where real estate's short-term status is either flat or depreciating. Keeping cash on hand and debt to a minimum was the name of the game in the Wilson household.

That's why these folks were such great candidates for a HECM. Convincing them of that took some education, however, since they originally approached a lender about taking out a traditional mortgage for a new home in Washington. They'd be moving from Colorado, where they'd just sold their family home for a neat profit of $419,400.

The Wilsons were familiar with traditional mortgages, hence their strong interest in using one on their new $427,000 home in Washington. But they didn't want to finance the whole cost of the home; they simply wanted a small loan of $50,000 and would pay for the remainder in cash. The Wilsons wanted to use the extra cash for home improvements, furniture, and to spruce up the Washington home to their liking.

So they started down the road to a traditional mortgage. A few minutes into the conversation a light bulb went on above the mortgage lenders head (no really, it actually did in this case!). These folks would be prime candidates for a HECM for purchase loan. Instead of forking over $407,000 in cash for the new home they'd be able to put down about $162,000 and save the rest of the their money for more important things like; additional liquidity, safety, and security. Even better: they wouldn't have a mortgage payment!

The idea of retaining half of the proceeds from their house and still not generate a new monthly mortgage payment made the Wilsons sit up and listen more closely. "How can that be possible?" they asked. "What kind of program could possibly be out there that would allow us to do this?"

Even as financially savvy as these homeowners were, the Wilsons were completely unaware of their HECM options (we see many of these cases – which is why I wrote this book in the first place). They had no idea that due to their age they could live in their new home with no mortgage payments. Should they decide to move from the property permanently and/or sell it, the mortgage balance (plus any accrued interest) would be due.

"But, this sounds a lot like a HECM," Todd said. "Won't I lose my property?" It was clear at this point that the Wilsons – much like many other senior homeowners – had received misinformation about today's HECMs. The lender explained that unlike the 1980s HECMs they didn't have to worry about losing the title to their home. In fact, they would retain title just like they would on the traditional mortgage. And at the same time they gained the advantage of knowing that there was no way foreclosure could ever happen to them, since the HECM was a non-recourse loan.

Todd understood what non-recourse meant. "So we're not personally liable for this loan, wow," he said, and then asked how the HECM would work. The lender explained that the loan balance would grow over time. Assuming that the home appreciated annually – and despite the current market – within five to 10 years they would see an increase in that balance. The Wilsons would keep the cash and any equity in the home (should they decide to sell) and put a lot less money down than they expected.

Solving the Problem

Being someone who understood the value of having cash on hand, Todd caught onto the concept fairly quickly and asked to sign up. The lender felt great to be able to help the Wilsons exceed their financial goals through basic education and the introduction of a viable, useful mortgage option: the HECM.

The HECM also assuaged another issue that the Wilsons were facing: turning over proofs of income and income tax returns and going through a full credit report. These things would be necessary for a traditional mortgage, but a HECM requires only that the Wilsons be of a certain age and have equity in the Washington home that they were purchasing.

"That's all we're interested in," The lender told Todd. "It's that simple" He was floored. Why isn't everyone doing this type of loan? He told him that he hears that from a lot of consumers and pointed out that the principals of the HECM were simple: you keep your cash and there's no monthly payment. The main difference from other loans is the timing of payments and how they are made.

As you can probably guess, they got the HECM processed and put the Wilsons in their new home for a $162,000 down payment and no monthly payment. They didn't have to fork over all of their financial documents and tax returns, nor did they have to make any new financial sacrifices as a result of their state-to-state move. It was a definite win for this pair of homeowners, who are now enjoying their steady monthly income and the knowledge that their bank account is now fatter than it's ever been!

Let's Do the Math

Todd and Joan Wilson didn't come to the lender in dire financial straits, nor were they looking for relief from high debts or the threat of foreclosure. They just needed a traditional mortgage on a new home. What they didn't realize is that there was a much better option waiting for them. Here's how they used a HECM for purchase to exceed their financial goals:

They sold their home in Colorado free and clear for:	$450,000
After sales expenses the net cash was:	$419,400
Purchase price for the Washington home:	$427,000
Age of the youngest borrower:	67
Maximum cash available from HECM for Purchase:	$225,600
Cash from borrower:	$200,400
Mortgage Insurance Premium:	$10,675
Financing fees and other costs:	$3,699
Cash now available from strategy:	**$219,000**

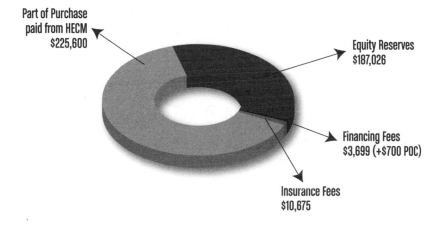

Part of Purchase paid from HECM $225,600

Equity Reserves $187,026

Financing Fees $3,699 (+$700 POC)

Insurance Fees $10,675

Tane's Take on It

Using the "Double Your Retirement Dollars Strategy" the Wilsons were able to keep an enormous amount of extra cash to be used for retirement. The extra cash will provide liquidity, safety, and security. A major concern of many retirees is long-term care and safety of principal. The Wilsons can use the extra funds to purchase safe guaranteed investments and long-term care insurance.

The American Medical Association performed a study that showed people who live to age 65 have a 50 percent chance of living another 25 years! The Wilsons can rest assured knowing they won't need to be greeters at Wal-Mart or asking you the question "paper or plastic?" at the supermarket. They have enough cash coupled with their additional assets and income to live another 25 years in comfort...do you?

How to Estimate the Down Payment for a HECM Purchase

Here's a simple formula for determining the required down payment for a HECM purchase. The formula is only an estimate and you should seek a professional HECM consultant or real estate professional that has a complete understanding of the program, and the software to run the calculations.

In this example we will be determining the down payment for a 62-year-old and a purchase price of $250,000.

Purchase price:	$250,000
Age of Youngest Borrower:	62
Subtract 10 from age:	(62-10) = 52

Determine the estimated loan amount of the HECM

Multiply .52 x sales price

.52 X $250,000 =   **$130,000**

Determine the Estimated Down Payment for the HECM Purchase

Subtract the sales price from the loan amount to calculate the down payment

($250,000-$130,000) =   **$120,000**

Below is a sample calculation that illustrates a purchase price of $250,000 where the youngest borrower is 62. The illustration displays an adjustable rate, meaning the rate can go up or down depending on market rates. The illustration shows how much equity is being used to pay the interest over the life of the loan by comparing the equity column year over year. Notice in year 10 the borrower could sell the house and have $148,796 in equity. The illustration assumes a 4% properly appreciation rate.

Annual Totals

Yr	Age	SVC Fee	Cash Payment	MIP	Rate
1	80	$0	$0	$1,842	2.990%
2	81	$0	$0	$1,921	2.990%
3	82	$0	$0	$2,004	2.990%
4	83	$0	$0	$2,091	2.990%
5	84	$0	$0	$2,182	2.990%
6	85	$0	$0	$2,276	2.990%
7	86	$0	$0	$2,374	2.990%
8	87	$0	$0	$2,477	2.990%
9	88	$0	$0	$2,584	2.990%
10	**89**	**$0**	**$0**	**$2,696**	**2.990%**
11	90	$0	$0	$2,812	2.990%
12	91	$0	$0	$2,934	2.990%
13	92	$0	$0	$3,061	2.990%
14	93	$0	$0	$3,193	2.990%
15	94	$0	$0	$3,331	2.990%
16	95	$0	$0	$3,475	2.99 0%
17	96	$0	$0	$3,625	2.990%
18	97	$0	$0	$3,782	2.990%
19	98	$0	$0	$3,946	2.990%
20	99	$0	$0	$4,116	2.990%

End of Year Projections

Interest	Loan Balance	Line Of Credit	Property Value	Equity
$4,406	$150,747	$0	$260,000	$108,628
$4,596	$157,265	$0	$270,400	$112,510
$4,795	$164,064	$0	$281,216	$116,527
$5,002	$171,157	$0	$292,465	$120,683
$5,218	$178,557	$0	$304,163	$124,982
$5,444	$186,278	$0	$316,330	$129,428
$5,679	$194,330	$0	$328,983	$134,028
$5,925	$202,731	$0	$342,142	$138,786
$6,181	$211,496	$0	$355,828	$143,707
$6,448	**$220,640**	**$0**	**$370,061**	**$148,796**
$6,727	$230,179	$0	$384,864	$154,059
$7,018	$240,131	$0	$400,258	$159,503
$7,321	$250,512	$0	$416,268	$165,131
$7,638	$261,343	$0	$432,919	$170,951
$7,968	$272,642	$0	$450,236	$176,969
$8,312	$284,429	$0	$468,245	$183,191
$8,672	$296,726	$0	$486,975	$189,624
$9,047	$309,555	$0	$506,454	$196,275
$9,438	$322,938	$0	$526,712	$203,150
$9,846	$336,900	$0	$547,781	$210,256

In the next chapter we'll explore just how valuable a HECM can be for consumers who want to purchase homes, but can't qualify for traditional loans due to poor credit or low incomes. They are over 62 years old…what can they do? You'll find out in Chapter Six.

Four Things to Remember from Chapter Five:

1. HECMs can be extremely useful financial planning tools for affluent retirees.

2. Senior homebuyers need only be the right age and have equity in their homes to be able to buy a home without a monthly mortgage payment.

3. No paystubs, income tax returns, or credit checks are needed when taking out a HECM.

4. HECMs for purchase allow homeowners to retain a high amount of cash when selling their homes to purchase new properties.

Want to find out how buying a home using a HECM Purchase is right for you?
Visit doubleyourretirementdollars.com/purchasequiz

For a more detailed video explanation please visit
doubleyourretirementdollars.com/purchasevideo

CHAPTER 6:

I Don't Qualify for a New Home Purchase Because of My Poor Credit, Income, and Lack of Down Payment

Low income levels, poor credit scores, lack of down payment resources, and past bankruptcies can all wreak havoc on a consumer's ability to buy a home via a traditional mortgage. The climate has gotten even tougher over the last few years as lenders pick up the pieces after the real estate downturn and the financial mess that it left behind.

Just a few years ago, for example, all it took to get a 100 percent, no-money-down mortgage was a pulse and a desire for homeownership. That's no longer the case. Lenders have tightened their standards and are once again qualifying only the buyers that can prove beyond a doubt that they can carry – and pay for – the burden of owning a home.

Buyers who are 62 years or older have more options at their avail, as Susan Turner recently learned. Told many times over that there was no way that she would qualify for a traditional mortgage, Susan was forced to live in a home that was in disrepair and expensive to heat and cool. The home was also too big for Susan, who had lived there for 40 years and wanted a change of scenery and a new life in a more manageable abode.

Susan's real estate agent unfortunately wasn't much help in this situation. She told Susan that a home loan was out of the question and – to prove what she was saying was true – referred the distraught homeowner to a traditional mortgage loan officer.

That loan officer pulled Susan's credit and uncovered a score of 587 – very poor. A mortgage lender would turn the other cheek, the officer told her, unless she had a very high down payment (which, of course, she did not – otherwise she would probably have been more creditworthy). The report revealed Susan's late mortgage payments, delinquent car payments, late credit card bills, several unpaid medical bills, and a few other negative marks. She'd been unable to cover those expenses, which had become a hardship for her.

Susan's situation probably sounds familiar to you. In fact, you may know some Susans – men and women who start paying their bills late with every intention of getting "back to normal" as quickly as possible. A few months go by and before they know it, their postal mailboxes are stuffed with dozens of late payment notices and their voice mailboxes are filled with collection calls.

So, back to Susan's plight. Due to circumstances that are now beyond her control, Susan's credit is terrible. She doesn't have a job and lives off a very low Social Security income. "I really can't help you at all," the loan officer told her. "Even an FHA program, which is designed for people who have low down payments and undesirable credit, won't work for you. The numbers just don't add up, sorry."

Susan walked away from that meeting assuming that she'd be stuck in her current home forever. She would *never* be able to buy a more comfortable, efficient home. Her heating and cooling bills would continue to mount and the list of repairs that needed tending to would only get longer. Poor Susan was disheartened, to say the least.

Solving the Problem

Down but not out, Susan was browsing the Internet one day and started reading an article about HECMs. She learned that based on her age and current ownership status, she could perhaps take out a HECM on her current home and use the proceeds to fix up the property, make it more efficient, and maybe even turn the basement into a rental unit (like a duplex). Susan was enthralled at the idea, but after thinking it through decided that getting out of the house completely and starting fresh would be an even better strategy.

Susan called a HECM consultant, who walked her through her options. The consultant explained the HECM for purchase program, which would allow Susan to buy a home that she wouldn't necessarily qualify for through traditional means, due to her poor credit and low income. After being told "no" so many times, Susan was nearly in tears with excitement at that point. She wanted to sign up right there, on the spot. A real estate agent was called in – along with Susan's children – and everyone sat down in a meeting to learn about the HECM program. The family's eyes lit up when they realized that their mom was going to literally get a new lease on life by getting out from under the expensive, burdensome home she'd been living in for four decades.

For her new home, Susan selected a 55-plus subdivision in Seattle. Being single, she was interested in meeting other mature homeowners and socializing over cards and tennis games. She purchased a new model home in the development.

The 1,900-square-foot, 3-bedroom/2-bath home was partially furnished and featured granite countertops, a single-level living area, and an energy efficient gas furnace and hot water heater. The home's kitchen was large and came with stainless steel appliances. The yard required very little maintenance, which meant Susan would no longer have to toil through the grass and weeds every week, doing upkeep. Instead, she could spend her time on better things.

Susan bought the home for $319,000 and used the proceeds from the sale of her old home to put down approximately 50 percent of the total cost of the new property. Her old, dilapidated house sold for $260,000 and Susan netted $243,100 after sales commissions and closing costs. Even after shelling out the down payment for her new home, Susan had plenty of cash left over ($90,222) to catch up on her credit card and medical bills and still save some for retirement.

These are things that Susan couldn't do before because she had no cash on hand. By paying her bills she's improving her credit score and also getting her creditors off her back. It's a great feeling for someone who has struggled financially for so long.

The news gets even better: Susan now lives in a new home and has no mortgage payment. Her monthly expenses are lower than ever thanks to the reduced utility bills. These reduced monthly expenses have freed up even more cash for Susan, who can invest in herself and even take the occasional vacation with friends, knowing that she's covered.

Let's Do the Math

In Susan's case – and so many other situations – participating in the HECM program made perfect sense. It solves a long-term problem that wasn't likely to go away anytime soon and vastly improved the quality of life to enjoy her surroundings and friends without stress and worry.

Here's the scenario for Susan Turner's HECM for purchase:

Susan's home (owned free and clear) sold for:	$260,000
After sales expenses her net cash was:	$243,100
Purchase price of home in Seattle:	$319,000
Age of the borrower:	66
Maximum cash available from HECM for Purchase:	$166,122
Down payment and closing costs from borrower:	$152,878
Mortgage Insurance Premium:	$7,975
Cash from "double your retirement dollars":	$90,222
"Bonus" - average monthly savings on utility bills	$137.09

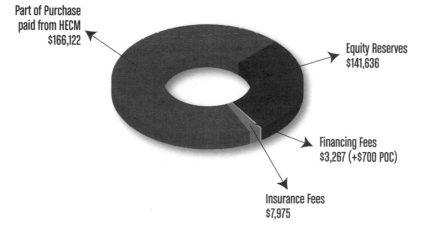

Part of Purchase paid from HECM $166,122

Equity Reserves $141,636

Financing Fees $3,267 (+$700 POC)

Insurance Fees $7,975

Tane's Take on It

Susan literally realized all of her financial goals – and all with no monthly mortgage payment. How great is that? Using the "Double Your Retirement Dollars Strategy" she was able to reserve $90,222 for her retirement needs and expenses. Had she stayed in the home that was in disrepair she would still have no savings, she'd be paying high utility expenses, and she would be unhappy and anxious. Talk about solving a lot of problems at once!

For people who don't currently own a home and have all but given up on it because of credit and income, don't fret. There now is an answer assuming there is money for a down payment. The HECM for purchase can help achieve the once unachievable.

In the next chapter you'll learn how grandparents can use HECMs to help their grandchildren – who wouldn't qualify for traditional mortgages – achieve the dream of homeownership.

Four Things to Remember from Chapter Six:

1. HECMs fill an important need for seniors who are age 62 or more.

2. Even poor credit histories and low income levels are okay when a senior is taking out a HECM for purchase.

3. HECMs can help seniors move into more desirable housing without monthly mortgage payments.

4. Using HECMs for purchase, homeowners can afford high down payments and still have ample cash on hand to be able to enjoy life with.

Susan considered turning her home into a duplex by renting out the basement before learning about the HECM for purchase. Purchasing a multifamily property is an excellent way to create rental income. The HECM for purchase will allow you to purchase up to a four-unit property provided you live in one of the units.

Want to find out how buying a duplex, triplex or fourplex can "Double Your Dollars" and increase your income?

Visit doubleyourretirementdollars.com/multifamily

CHAPTER 7:

Helping Your Grandchildren Buy a Home

Most of the U.S. real estate markets are veritable candy stores for homebuyers and investors right now. The landscape isn't expected to change dramatically anytime soon. According to Realtor.com, there were 1.89 million homes on the market at the end of December 2011. And while the numbers represented a 22.3% decline compared to 2010, that's still a lot of properties for sale. With many of them either in (or teetering on the edge of) foreclosure or eligible for short sale status, the prices are right for buyers who are ready, willing, and able to buy.

The problem is that many of those would-be buyers are looking for their first homes. They are facing very tight credit standards, extremely difficult underwriting regulations, and a mortgage market that's still dealing with the after effects of the secondary mortgage market implosion. We already went over this in detail in the last chapter, but put simply: financing just isn't as easy to come by as it was a few years ago.

To qualify for loans, today's buyers have to really bring their best game to the table. They have to have good income levels, high credit scores, and enough cash to cover a respectable down payment. And while many first-time homebuyers qualify for loans on the merits of their income or credit scores, coming up with the down payment money isn't always easy.

Some FHA programs allow buyers to put just 3 percent down on their new homes, but these programs are expensive. For example, when the down payment is less than 20 percent of the home's cost, buyers have to figure in the high cost of mortgage insurance premiums, both in terms of a lump sum, upfront fee, and monthly payments. Those payments can reach ridiculous amounts like $200 to $500 or more. To make the situation even more challenging, that mortgage insurance most cases is not tax deductable.

The end result is usually a homeowner whose income just doesn't cover all of the housing expenses.

Solving the Problem

Here's a story about a recent challenging situation with a young couple in Nashville. In their mid-20s, Brian and Melissa Johnson had their hearts set on a starter home that was priced at $247,000. It was a nice property that should have conceivably been affordable for two people who had good jobs and good credit scores. They should have qualified for conventional financing...but they lacked the necessary cash for a down payment.

As newlyweds, the Johnsons did what a lot of young couples are doing these days: they spent most of their available cash on their wedding. They wanted a home of their own, but didn't have the time needed to save up for a down payment. They tried to qualify for an FHA loan, but the mortgage premium was so high that it put their home of choice out of reach.

Brian and Melissa only had $3,000 in the bank, but they weren't ready to give up yet. They talked to their mortgage broker about alternative ways to come up with down payments, including gifts from friends and/or relatives. In fact, the mortgage broker suggested that they call their parents – or anyone else they knew, like a rich uncle – to raise the money for the down payment (which was $57,000, or 20 percent of the $247,000 home purchase price plus closing costs). That way, they'd be able to avoid mortgage insurance altogether – both on the front end and in terms of the monthly payments.

So the Johnsons started asking around. They talked to their parents and grandparents, including Mary Johnson, an 87-year-old retired federal employee of 35 years. Mary gets a nice monthly income pension of $4,120 per month but really doesn't have any extra cash. Brian still wanted to talk to her about helping with the down payment.

Mary was born in Nazi Germany. She was 10 years old when she escaped the country and moved to the U.S. where she became a naturalized citizen. She worked as a federal employee for most of her life and understands the value and freedom of being able to buy your own home. She's interested in helping her grandson and granddaughter-in-law to the extent that she can – even if it means letting them borrow the money they need to buy their own home.

"I need $57,000," Brian said to his grandmother, who gave him a puzzled look. "I don't have that kind of cash," she responded. He explained to her that he'd been reading up on HECMs and how the equity in her home could be liquidated in the form of cash, which he and Melissa would then put into their own home.

Looking for more information about HECMs, Mary approached me for help. She wanted to see Brian and Melissa live in their own home. She wanted to be able to go and visit them on holidays and weekends in their new home now, while she was alive and vibrant. Having them benefit from her home equity *after* she was gone was of no interest to Mary. She wanted to do something now, while she could enjoy the benefits of the purchase as well.

Mary was an easy client to work with because she understood the value of sharing her wealth with younger generations while she was still alive. "It's better to give with a warm hand," Mary said. "From the grave, I won't be able to experience the joy of seeing my grandson living in and enjoying his new home."

The HECM consultant and real estate agent for Brian and Melissa sat down with Mary and explained exactly how the HECM process and purchase worked. They told her that she'd receive enough cash from her $180,000 home to meet her grandson's down payment needs. She'd also never have a mortgage payment on the home that she plans to live in for the rest of her life. The situation was ideal and allowed two different generations of the Johnson family to achieve their goals in a painless, seamless fashion.

Let's Do the Math

When Mary handed Brian and Melissa a check for $57,000 to cover their down payment and closing costs, the newlyweds' faces lit up like Christmas trees. It had all happened so quickly and without much intervention on their part – they couldn't even believe their eyes! Mary gifted her grandson the money as part of his inheritance (which he would have gotten anyway) and was then able to sit back and watch the couple enjoy their beautiful new home.

Here's the scenario for Mary Johnson for a HECM that provided her grandson a $57,000 down payment:

Value of Mary's home:	$180,000
Age of the borrower:	87
Maximum cash available from HECM:	$75,821
Mortgage Insurance Premium	$900
Financing fees and other costs:	$2,011 (+$700 POC)
Gift to grandson for purchase of new home	
(Advancing the inheritance):	$57,000

Extra Cash available from "double your retirement dollars strategy": **$18,821**

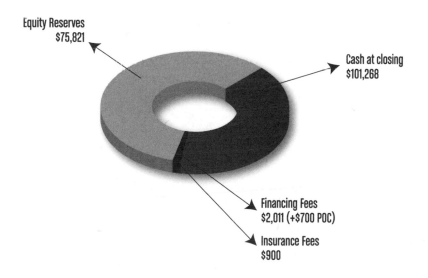

Equity Reserves
$75,821

Cash at closing
$101,268

Financing Fees
$2,011 (+$700 POC)

Insurance Fees
$900

Tane's Take on It

Using the "Double Your Dollars Strategy" Mary Johnson was able to advance her inheritance to her grandson to purchase a home in a strong buyer's market. Because they put down 20 percent of the home's price as a down payment, Brian and Melissa got the best financing and avoided mortgage insurance fees. Mary can now enjoy seeing her grandson in his new home while she is alive – talk about giving with a warm hand.

In Part II of this book we'll switch gears and start looking at how you can use equity conversion for estate planning, beginning with a scenario that shows how a consumer can retire at 62 and still maximize his social security benefits. If you're ready to hear how this can be done using a HECM, turn the page to Chapter Eight.

Four Things to Remember from Chapter Seven:

1. First-time homebuyers with solid incomes and good credit scores are often challenged by a lack of substantial down payment funds.

2. Senior homebuyers often don't realize the assets that they are sitting on in their homes that are fully paid off.

3. HECMs are a great way for homeowners over the age of 62 to distribute advanced inheritance funds to their children and/or grandchildren.

4. When homeowners use HECMs to liquidate equity they do not incur any new monthly mortgage payments.

Using Equity Management to Increase Income, Social Security Benefits, and Estate Planning

CHAPTER 8:

It's All About –
Liquidity and Safety

Congratulations! You've made it to retirement. Now that you have plenty of cash saved in your 401(k) and IRA you are ready start living the good life. The kids are grown, the job is gone, and the RV is ready to roll out of the driveway and into the sunset.

Not so fast. How has your plan worked out? Do you have enough money to be able to safely withdraw on your retirement funds? What about your home – did you pay it off just like you were taught at a young age? That's right – paying off your home was one of the basic tenets that your parents probably taught you right along with,

1. Get a good education

2. Get a good job that you retire from in 30-plus years

3. Buy a home and pay it off

4. And then, retire!

Sixty-seven percent of Americans aged 65+ own their homes free and clear. These folks are sitting on, lying in, cooking in, and watching TV in trillions of dollars in equity. But what's the home equity doing for them? Sure it provides peace of mind that no one can take their homes away from them. They are free from the anxiety that they could be on the street and homeless – an especially relevant topic in today's real estate market.

The problem is that from a financial point of view, these seniors are sitting on assets that do absolutely nothing for them. They are missing out on the liquidity, safety, and rate of return that they'd gain by taking out HECMs on their homes. Put simply – and despite what your parents may have taught you – accumulating equity can actually be a bad idea.

Let's examine the assertion that equity can be bad:

Every prudent investment must have three key elements. First it must provide liquidity. Can you get the money whenever you want? Is it guaranteed or insured against loss of principal and finally what rate of return does it provide?

Look closely at the following investment and determine how much money you would like to invest. Here are the elements of the investment:

1. You decide the amount and length of time for the monthly contributions to continue.

2. You can pay more than the minimum monthly contribution, but not less.

3. If you attempt to pay less, the financial institution keeps all the previous contributions.

4. The money deposited into the account is not safe from loss of principal.

5. Each contribution made to the account results in less safety.

6. The money in the account is not liquid if you need it.

7. It earns a zero rate of return.

8. When the plan if fully funded there is no income paid out.

Doesn't sound like a very good option, does it? Yet it's a house with the traditional mortgage – an investment pick that millions of Americans have made, never fully understanding the negative impact that it will have on their nest eggs.

A home that's completely paid off and no longer tied to a traditional mortgage is similar to a 401(k), IRA, or any other retirement account that was funded with consistent, monthly contributions over the years. Working hard your entire life to own your home outright is admirable, but consumers can take their investment to a new level by viewing it less emotionally as a balance sheet asset and then tapping into it. Then will the homeowner be able to gain additional freedom and options by creating a "home" retirement account that they never thought of before.

The Return On Equity is ALWAYS Zero

Home equity is defined as the difference between the mortgage balance and the home's market value. If you have a home that is worth $300,000, and if you owe $50,000 on a mortgage, then your home equity is $300,000 - $50,000 for a net figure of $250,000 in home equity.

Market Value - Mortgage Balance = Home Equity

I am sure if you were to tell me what kind of return you are getting on your retirement investments you would be able to provide a pretty accurate answer. However if I were to ask you the return on your home equity, how would you answer? Would you say -10% since home values are going down? What about when home prices where increasing at an unprecedented pace? What was your home equity then? If home values were increasing 10% per year, would your home equity be increasing by 10%?

Surprisingly the answer is no, and here's why:

> An increase or decrease in a home's equity does *not* equate to the homeowner earning a rate of return on the equity. If you own your home free and clear and your home increases in value by $50,000, you'll have that much more equity within a year.

> If you have no equity in the same home and the value increases by $50,000, you still have an increase in the equity amount of $50,000. It doesn't matter if you have a mortgage or no mortgage both scenarios provide an increase of an additional $50,000.

> Carrying a mortgage does not change anything; the rate of return on your equity is zero. There is no interest earned on equity in a home, whether it's owned free and clear or mortgaged to the hilt. The bank doesn't "pay" you interest payments for being a good customer and paying off your home. The equity in your home is idle and does nothing to benefit you financially.

How many people have seen their equity evaporate over the last few years and only wish they have separated their equity? I know several owners whose $1 million+ homes are now worth

$400,000 or $500,000. Can you imagine a loss of $500,000 in your investment portfolio? It would be devastating for even the most affluent families.

Do you remember a time in the 1980s when the Texas oil boom went bust and many people lost their homes to foreclosure? Had they removed equity from their home before prices went down they could have used some of the cash on hand to pay the mortgage. They could have weathered the storm.

Now think about the current real estate drop, and how homeowners in California, Arizona, Nevada, and Florida have experienced huge decreases in home prices. Values literally plummeted after going off the charts for several years. As a result, the country is now experiencing some of the highest foreclosure rates in history. I am sure many of these owners wish they'd been able to get their home equity converted into cash before the hammer fell.

Offsetting the Costs

By now you may be wondering about the cost of getting the equity out of your home and into liquid cash. After all, refinancing costs money, right? There are a number of factors to consider. A traditional mortgage will cost you fees, interest, and most importantly monthly payments. Think of the monthly payment as an "employment cost" or what it costs to remove the equity. The beauty of a HECM loan is that from a cash flow point of view there is no "employment cost" or monthly payment required. With a standard mortgage at 5 percent interest rate, for example, you will have a monthly out of pocket mortgage payment and a need to place the cash in a safe investment and generate a reasonable rate of return.

However, with a HECM the rate may be around 5 percent, but with no monthly out of pocket employment cost. Keep in mind the interest is being added to the reverse balance and accruing against the equity but is insured against the balance ever becoming more than the value.

Since there is no out of pocket monthly payment the HECM is ideal for creating safety and liquidity without burdening your monthly cash flow. You or your heirs will not be responsible for balance in excess of the value. If you have a current mortgage, that debt can be converted from full recourse to non-recourse HECM removing your personal liability. Here are some prudent and creative ways to provide liquidity and safety using a HECM, which we'll discuss in further detail in the coming chapters:

— Maximize Social Security benefits by bridging the gap between age 62 and 70.

— Minimize withdrawal from your taxable retirement accounts and use the equity tax-free.

— Keep investment growing and maturing and not be forced to use the money if the timing isn't right.

— Offset taxable withdrawals from IRAs through liquid equity.

— Create additional income by investing in rental property with no money out of pocket and no payments.

— Build a plan to be sure you "age in place" and cover your long-term care needs into the future.

— Transfer wealth and create immediate income.

— Lock in equity now to preserve it for liquidity and safety.

— Create a legacy and transfer wealth tax-free in perpetuity.

There are other compelling reasons to get out of the "accumulate as much equity as possible" mindset. By separating the equity from our homes we transfer the risk to the lender. When you own your home free and clear you assume all the risk. If a natural disaster strikes or the house burns down, you lose the free and clear property and all the equity. Of course you have insurance coverage, but in many cases it won't cover the total cost to rebuild.

If the home is mortgaged to the hilt, however, with the equity separated in cash, you can sleep easier knowing that if your home burns to the ground, or if the value drops, you'll be well positioned. Remember: your home is a shelter and a place for memories but not a place to store all of your assets.

Tane's Take on It

This is one of the biggest hurdles for people to understand. Equity in a home is *not* a prudent investment yet many have fallen into the false sense of security. Be sure to grasp this truth to better appreciate the upcoming chapters.

Four Things to Remember from Chapter Eight

1. Accumulating equity in a home is *not* a profitable investment strategy.

2. Every prudent investment must – first and foremost – provide liquidity and safety.

3. It doesn't matter if your home is paid off or mortgaged to the hilt, it doesn't generate profits.

4. Separating your home's equity from your home is a very good idea especially in retirement when it makes the most sense.

CHAPTER 9:

How to Retire at 62 and Receive the Maximum Social Security Benefits

If the idea of retiring at 62 is attractive but out of reach because you won't be able to get the maximum Social Security benefits, think again. You may not have to keep working until you are 70 to reach that Holy Grail; you can bridge that 8-year age gap and maximize Social Security with a HECM.

Using a HECM to generate retirement income is a straightforward way for senior homeowners to tap into some or all of the wealth that's tied up in their homes. Yet surveys reveal that very few eligible borrowers have considered this route, assuming that the options will be out of reach for anyone with an inadequate cash flow or poor credit rating. In fact, as you've already learned from earlier chapters of this book, your income, assets, debts, and credit scores don't matter when you apply for a HECM.

With mature homeowners struggling to find the best way to cover their costs in a down economy, many have to decide between selling stock or utilizing HECMs. Personal finance guru Suze Orman recently gave advice to a homeowner who was facing this particular dilemma, and told the consumer that it was "better to hold onto stock investments and employ a HECM."

The rationale is clear: stocks are more likely to provide a larger profit and recoup their losses at a faster rate than the housing market, particularly in today's real estate environment. Theoretically, a homeowner's heir could be left with more money overall in 10 years, factoring in the stock and equity left in the house after the cost of the HECM is taken out.

HECMs can also solve the Social Security benefits conundrum that surfaces when you try to start collecting at age 62. Your social security income is reduced by a fraction of a percent for each month before your full retirement age (and increased by a percentage – depending on your birth date – if delayed past full retirement age) and then maxes out at age 70.

Waiting until you are 70 to collect Social Security benefits results in higher monthly benefit payments. But who wants to work full-time until the age of 70? That's right – no one! For homeowners with sufficient equity, a HECM can help bridge the 8-year cash flow gap. If you haven't already considered this move, think about it and talk to your financial advisors about your options. Use the U.S. Social Security Administration's website for the latest rules regarding retirement income payments.

Here are a few reasons why homeowners aged 62-69 would consider a HECM to generate retirement income:

— Most have greater life expectancies than their parents and aren't prepared to fund a lengthy retirement.

— Medical advancements have prolonged life expectancies into the 80's, 90's, and even 100's.

— These retirees are less likely to have pensions (than their parents did).

— Most of them haven't recovered from the most recent

stock market meltdown.

— More than half of all retirees have less than $25,000 in savings (source: Employee Benefit Research Institute).

— Those seniors who are 62 and ready to receive Social Security benefits will receive much smaller checks than if they waited until they were 65, 67, or even 70.

— Many of these folks want to start their retirement lifestyles *now*...not in eight years.

— They are trying to figure out a way to maximize the Social Security benefit while still having the benefit of retiring at 62.

By the Numbers

In June 2011, the Government Accountability Office (GAO) published a retirement income report entitled, "Ensuring Income Throughout Retirement Requires Difficult Choices." The report mentions the importance of not simply preparing for retirement, but also maintaining income during retirement. The problem is that Social Security is somewhat of a Ponzi scheme: eligible seniors get money from one investor (in this case tax payers are the investors) to pay off earlier investors (current social security recipients) in that scheme. Essentially, the government is getting money from young workers to pay off those who have already paid into the system because, unfortunately, the Social Security system by definition is bankrupt. Politicians realize the problem but continue to kick the proverbial can down the road while preserving their own career.

The GAO report suggests that Social Security's trust fund reserves will be exhausted by 2036 – one year earlier than expected. I think it will be even earlier because there simply aren't enough workers entering the workforce to pay the tax needed to continue funding. Making matters even more challenging, Medicare funds are expected to run out in 2024. Combined, these two issues alone create a pretty gloomy forecast for the nation's aging population.

But wait, there's more:

— According to a recent Gallup poll, 25 percent of seniors have burned through their personal life savings and are in bad shape for retirement.

— The Center for Retirement Research at Boston College developed a national retirement risk index, which projects that 51 percent of retiring households were at risk of being unable to maintain their preretirement standard of living in 2009.

— The GAO reports that 62.1 percent of Americans take Social Security benefits shortly after the 62nd birthdays and 72.8 percent are taking benefits before they hit 65.

The GAO report urges seniors to delay their Social Security benefits as long as possible (but not past 70, since that would lead to additional reductions in distributions) in order to receive higher benefit amounts. The organization also recommends that seniors draw down their savings and either convert a portion of their savings into an income annuity that would cover expenses or choose an annuity plan sponsored by an employer.

Bridging the Gap

HECMs are a great way to bridge the gap and help retirees enjoy their senior years with much less stress and hassle. Don and Angie Young, a married couple from Traverse City, Mich., learned this firsthand when they both decided to retire at the age of 62. Prior to leaving their jobs, Don was earning $87,000 annually and Angie was bringing home $32,000 a year. To figure out how much Social Security they would be eligible for, the Youngs – who own a $625,000 home free and clear – visited the administration's website and inputted their salary information.

Using the online calculator, Angie figured out that she was eligible to receive $763 per month or $9,156 annually. After finding out the figures she decided to start taking her social security benefits. Next they checked out Don's eligibility. He'd worked most of his life while Angie worked raising the children, so he was eligible for more benefits. Don was eligible for $1,476 a month or $17,712 per year. Assuming cost of living adjustments included in the social security benefits calculations, by the time Don reaches age 70 he will receive the maximum benefit of $1,751 or $20,017 per year.

If Don waited to collect Social Security until he turns 70, however, his annual benefits would nearly double to $39,504. Waiting would bring some significant benefits, but the Youngs really had their hearts set on retiring from work and enjoying the rest of their years together, without having to work.

The Youngs had another ace up their sleeves: a lot of home equity in the property they'd owned for decades. They spoke with their financial advisor, who in turn introduced them to a knowledgeable HECM consultant. That consultant realized that a HECM Line of Credit would be the best bet for this married couple, based on the option's low-cost mortgage insurance premium.

Let's Do the Math

The HECM Line of Credit is comparable to a traditional home equity line. It's a loan against the property, but it's both easy to qualify for and competitive in interest charges. Unlike a traditional HELOC (Home Equity Line of Credit) senior homeowners can enjoy the freedom of no payments.

With the HECM Line of Credit there are no income or credit requirements; the closing costs are reasonably low; the interest rates are competitive; there are no prepayment penalties; and the credit line is guaranteed. In fact the credit line will increase each year on the unused portion, giving access to additional funds. The current program includes a credit line growth rate that will continue regardless even if your home appreciates in value. With the credit line growth you will gain increased access to more equity on any amount of the credit line you don't access.

The option was very attractive for the Youngs, who would benefit greatly by deferring Social Security payments until Don reached the age of 70. They withdrew $21,684 annually from the HECM (or $1,807 per month) and collected that amount for eight years (on top of Angie's Social Security income). Don stopped collecting on the HECM when he turned 70, and Angie stopped receiving her Social Security income the same year (because she could collect more as a "spouse" under Don's Social Security plan).

When the Youngs stopped drawing on their HECM the balance on their HECM Line of Credit was $180,635 assuming rates remain constant. They now can begin drawing more from their retirement accounts. The Young's retirement accounts are taxable but they can offset any tax burden if needed, by paying interest on the HECM Line of Credit. The interest is tax deductible on the HECM once they pay the interest and can be used for advanced tax planning purposes.

Don, whose life expectancy is 84 years, will receive an actual benefit from Social Security of $641,029 (pretax). Because he waited until 70 to tap into those benefits his lifetime benefit increased from $440,374 to $641,029 – an amazing increase of $200,655, compared to the amount he would have netted if he'd started taking distributions at age 62.

That deferral was a no-brainer for the Youngs, who were not only able to kick off their retirement in style while just 62 years old, but they were also able to pocket over $200,000 in additional monies in the process. The HECM provided liquidity outside of Social Security and was a prudent move for this couple. The scenarios don't always play out the same way and should be assessed on a case-by-case basis. In many situations, however the end results are extremely positive for the homeowners.

Here's the HECM scenario for Don and Angie Young that provided them with retirement income and bridged the gap between 62 and 70 to maximize Social Security benefits through HECM Line of Credit payments:

Home Value:	$625,000
Age of youngest borrower:	62
HECM Line of Credit proceeds available:	$311,703
Mortgage Insurance Premium:	$3,125
Other closing costs:	$2,609
Monthly Tenure Payment Received:	$1,807
Balance at the end of 8 years when Don is 70:	$180,635

Tane's Take on It

The benefits of waiting for Social Security are so great that it pays to consider all alternative options *before* joining the high percentage of Americans who tap into this financial source the minute they turn 62. What many of these individuals don't realize is that over $3 trillion that the 62-plus crowd has accumulated in home equity (according to the National Reverse Mortgage Lenders Association's most recent numbers) can easily serve as a viable income stream while they wait for the big "7-0" to come along.

In the next chapter we'll take the retirement account deferral strategy a step further and show you how you can retire in style *without* having to sell your investment assets.

Four Things to Remember from Chapter Nine

1. 25 percent of seniors have burned through their personal life savings and are in bad shape for retirement.

2. Using a HECM to generate retirement income is a straightforward way for senior homeowners to tap into some or all of the wealth that's tied up in their homes.

3. Most retirees have less than $25,000 in savings (source: Age Wave, agewave.com).

4. HECM Lines of Credit allow homeowners to use HECMs as an alternative to a standard line of credit but with no monthly payments or traditional qualifying.

CHAPTER 10:

How to Delay Withdrawing Retirement Funds Allowing Them to Grow and Still Retire in Style

Most people who have retired in recent years or those looking to do so in the near future are looking at very different nest eggs than the ones they had 10 years ago. The stock market drop of 2008 and the subsequent volatility have put retirees and near-retirees in a precarious position. Not only have their accounts lost significant value, but any chance of reaping high returns and recouping those losses is difficult at best.

Out of sheer fear of losing their life's savings, many people have tried to time the market by pulling their assets out of stocks and putting them into bonds (when a drop is eminent) and then taking the opposite approach when things are looking rosy. This activity can have a long-term, negative impact on a portfolio thanks to high transaction costs and the basic fact that *no one* can time the stock market. By managing their own accounts and operating in this manner many people have lost more than they should have during the recent stock market downturn.

Exacerbating the problem is the fact that when investors review their returns over the last five years, the numbers are much lower than they assume. There's a grey area when you are assessing "average" annualized returns. Let's say an investment went up 100 percent one year and dropped 50 percent the next. You might say you had a net gain of 50%. You certainly wouldn't say you had a gain of 25 percent. However, if we address the actual return we need to look at the simple average or the arithmetic mean while 0 percent is the geometric mean (annualized return or compound annual growth rate [CAGR]).

Volatile investments are often expressed using the simple average rather than the CAGR, which is actually smaller. Here's an example of how this works:

> For the 5-year time frame between January 1, 2006 and December 31, 2011, the average return on the S&P 500 was 4.67 percent. Now that doesn't seem so bad until you look at the CAGR, which was 2.23 percent. That's much lower and equates to $1.14 on a $1.00 investment over a 5-year period.

Many investors lost a lot of money trying to time the market putting money in bonds when the market dropped, then investing in stocks again when the coast seemed clear. If you stuck it out and kept your money in stocks you were making 2.23 percent – hardly enough to cultivate a healthy retirement account but at least a positive return. Most are in a holding pattern having to wait it out and hope beyond hope that their investment grows quickly.

That's the situation that Steven and Rochelle Miller were in. At one time this married couple from Phoenix had $623,000 in combined Roth IRA and other investment accounts. When the market went south the Millers tried to time it and wound up with a nearly 50 percent reduction in their portfolio, which leveled off at about $387,000. It was a hard pill for the Millers to swallow, considering how long they'd worked to save for retirement. They were distraught over the loss, on the cusp of a retirement, and confused about what step to take next.

What the Millers had in their favor was an $875,000 home that was paid off in full. It was a godsend that they didn't even realize they were sitting on – and one that helped them recoup their financial losses. Their financial advisor mentioned the possibility of a HECM and pointed them in the direction of a consultant who would walk them through the details and get them set up on the road to recovery.

The HECM line of credit made the most sense for the Millers, who would gain access to the greatest amount of cash. Steven and Rochelle would gain the most benefits from a LIBOR-based (the average interest rate that leading banks in London charge when lending to other banks), indexed, adjustable HECM that would give them the flexibility to take out as much money as they wanted or needed and at any given time.

Let's Do the Math

The Millers used a HECM strategy that allowed them to draw down equity and only accrue interest when they made withdrawals. They decided to pay themselves $2,300 a month on a tax-free basis and without impacting their Medicare or Social Security wages.

The Millers were able to create a combined income of about $4,700 a month. The Social Security portion was taxable but it was also low. Add in the other tax deductions that they were entitled to and the Millers didn't have to pay any income taxes, and they won't until they start withdrawing from their IRAs – which can now grow in their "buy and hold" accounts that are no longer being moved around for fear of further principal reductions.

The best aspect of this story is that the Millers can access their HECM cash flow for a long time to come. They are both 65 years old and the proceeds generated from the HECM equaled a total line of credit of $329,013. Their $2,300-a-month distributions will last over 13 years (or even more if their home value increases). To say the Millers have options is an understatement. This pair is in a much better financial position than they were pre-HECM and all because they discovered the untapped benefits of their paid-off home.

For example, they can stop the proceeds from the HECM at any time and take distributions from their IRA accounts. Even more importantly, they have liquidity in their IRAs *and* from the HECM. They are secure and can sleep at night knowing that their nest egg is not only safe, but that it's in "re-building" mode.

Here's how Steven and Rochelle kept their retirement assets invested and increasing by taking a HECM line of credit:

Home Value:	$875,000
Age of youngest borrower	65
Home Equity Conversion Mortgage Line of Credit:	$329,013
Mortgage Insurance Premium:	$3,127
Other closing costs:	$3,234

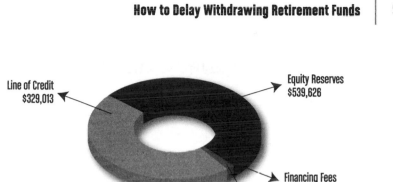

Line of Credit
$329,013

Equity Reserves
$539,626

Financing Fees
$2,609 (+$625 PNC)

Insurance Fees
$3,127

Exploring Lines of Credit

After reading about the Millers, you may be wondering: what if they didn't need to take withdrawals from their line of credit initially? The answer to that question opens up alternative possibilities for HECM borrowers. They could, for example, go ahead and open up a line of credit now and opt not to use it. So every year that amount of money would continue to grow. By the time the Millers turn 75 the line would equal $653,565 and if they wait until they are 85 to tap into it, the value of the line of credit will be over $1.3 million.

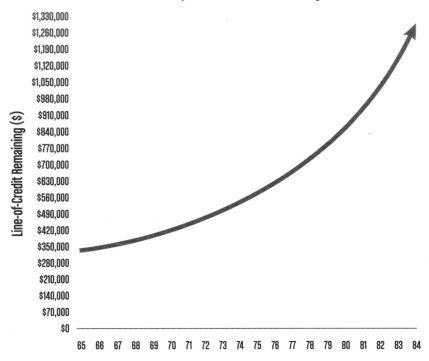

Projected Line-of-Credit Remaining

As you can see, using the line of credit strategy and then waiting to use that money would be an advantageous move for the Millers. And remember that credit line growth is *guaranteed* because any unused portion of the credit grows according to the pre-determined growth rate of current interest plus 1.25 percent (compare these rates to the average rate on a one-year CD, which was 0.24 percent in June 2014, and the average for a 5-year CD at the time was 0.78 percent, according to Bankrate.com). At any point, the Millers can request a withdrawal and get their money – no questions asked and with no tax ramifications. The HECM line of credit will never be canceled and is guaranteed to grow. (This is not to be confused with a rate of return on an investment.) If they let that money grow, it can serve as a great alternative for long-term care or any other myriad expenses that may come up. Put simply, a HECM line of credit can be a great way to set up a whole separate bucket of money for retirement.

In *A great reverse mortgage idea: Take a credit line now,* Jane Bryant Quinn writes, "With HECMS, you don't have to make monthly payments, as you do with a regular loan. The mortgage doesn't come due until you leave your home permanently. When the house is finally sold, the proceeds go first to repay what you borrowed, plus the accumulated interest. If there's money left over, it goes to you or your heirs. If the house sells for less than the loan amount, the Federal Housing Administration, which insures HECMs, covers the lender's loss."[1]

The growing line of credit is one of the most overlooked benefits of a HECM, the FHA program allows the homeowner's line of credit to grow at 125 (1.25%) basis points above the current loan interest rate. The option also offers:

— Equity protection because the funds are unaffected by fluctuations in home value

— A line of credit that doesn't count as an asset for government benefit programs

— Interest charged only on the money drawn from the line of credit

— Non-taxable growth

— Control over the timing and the amount of advances

— FHA insured-funds

1 Quinn, Janet Bryan, A great reverse mortgage idea: Take a credit line now, August 15, 2013.

In *Reversing the Conventional Wisdom: Using Home Equity to Supplement Retirement Income,* attorney Barry H. Sacks and professor Stephen R. Sacks, explored the results of adding a mortgage credit line to a HECM. In their report, the authors illustrated the cash flow survival probabilities when the reverse mortgage credit line is used in addition to the account, in all three strategies. The illustrative example uses the following input data:

— The initial account value is $800,000.15

— The home value is equal to the pre-2009 HECM limit of $417,000. (We are not aware of any reverse mortgages currently available that provide loans based on home values higher than the HECM limit and provide the loans in the form of a credit line.)

— The initial withdrawal rate is the primary variable used in our comparison of the three withdrawal strategies. We show results for initial withdrawal rates of 5.0 percent, 6.0 percent, and 6.5 percent.

— In this example, we assume the retiree is age 65, and the resulting credit line available is approximately $266,000 in the initial year at the current expected rate and approximately $183,000 at the 37-year mean expected rate. In both the reverse-mortgage-last strategy and the coordinated strategy, the reverse mortgage credit line is established later in the 30-year sequence, so the amount available is greater.

In considering this example, it is important to note that the home value used to determine the reverse mortgage amount is approximately equal to 52 percent of the account value. If the home value were lower, or the account value were higher, the ratio of home value to account value would be lower; as a result, the effect of the reverse mortgage credit line on the probability of cash flow survival would also be lower. "We show below a quantitative measure of the impact on our results of the ratio of home value to account value," the authors conclude, "both above and below this 52 percent ratio."

Tane's Take on It

Just to reiterate, one major problem with "average" investment returns is that there is real ambiguity about what people mean by "average." Volatile investments are frequently stated in terms of the simple average, rather than the CAGR that you actually get. (Bad news: the CAGR is smaller.) There are calculators online that help you pinpoint the annualized growth rate of the S&P 500 over the date range you specify; you'll find that the CAGR is usually about a percent or two less than the simple average.

This issue – combined with the stock market volatility and attempts to time the market – has left investors' retirement portfolios in shambles. Those at or near retirement were hit particularly hard in their attempts to salvage the bits of their nest eggs that are left. There's a bright light at the end of the tunnel for homeowners who are 62 and over: the HECM. As outlined in this chapter, it just makes sense for seniors to tap into their equity and use it to sustain themselves financially while their portfolios cure.

One option that provides safety and liquidity that is often overlooked is the availability of fixed-income guaranteed insurance-based products. Such products can be very attractive for providing safety and income guaranteed by top-rated insurance companies. Consult a financial advisor about such products and for help determining if they are right for you.

In the next chapter we'll look at another way that HECMs can be extremely valuable for homeowners by allowing them to transfer wealth and create immediate income for themselves.

Six Things to Remember from Chapter Ten

1. Timing the market is a bad idea that results in much lower portfolio values.

2. There's a big difference between "average" annual returns and CAGR. Rates of return quoted my major media sources of financial information use figures that can be deceiving.

3. Much like loans, certain HECM options allow you to draw down equity and only accrue interest when you make withdrawals.

4. A HECM can help homeowners sustain themselves financially while their retirement portfolios re-build.

5. The credit line growth rate on a HECM is one the most powerful features that few people know about

6. Investigate guaranteed return insurance-based products with an insurance agent or financial advisor that is well versed in these products.

CHAPTER 11:

How to Transfer Wealth and Create Immediate Income – A Super Charged Real Estate Strategy

As Ben Franklin wrote in a 1789 letter, *"In this world nothing can be said to be certain, except death and taxes."* More than 200 years later that statement still holds true. In fact, most would argue that the average tax bite is larger and even more punishing than it was when Franklin scribed those words in his letter to Jean Baptiste Le Roy.

Estate taxes bite particularly hard. Even the smallest of estates pay their fair share (or more, in some cases) of federal estate taxes (the highest federal tax bracket is 45 percent). The fact that many states also collect their own estate or inheritance taxes (those rates top out at 12 to 16 percent), can make the "final bill" even bigger. Those states typically set their estate tax threshold at $1 million, although some target lower levels and others hit only the largest estates.

The good news is that many estates *don't* owe these additional taxes because their owners distributed funds to their heirs while they were still alive, and/or transferred up to $5.12 million to others, pre-tax. This is known as the personal estate tax exemption and it allows a specific dollar amount of property to be passed on tax-free, regardless of who the recipient is.

The marital deduction is another ace in the hole for those who pass on and leave behind property and wealth. All property left to a surviving spouse passes to that person without the threat of estate tax, according to the IRS. Another estate planning tool is the family limited partnership (FLP), which helps to centralize family-held investments and/or businesses.

Using an FLP, taxpayers can combine those assets into one, family-owned business partnership. Family members own partnership shares and can transfer those shares to different generations of the family. The tool can be particularly useful in reducing taxes by transferring (a process known as "gifting") shares to younger generations that may be in lower tax brackets.

With an FLP, senior family members become "general partners" and then transfer some of their limited partnership ownership to beneficiaries (children, heirs, a trust, etc.). According to the IRS, the FLP must have a valid business reason and cannot be formed solely as a tax-reduction tool.

Since there's no way to avoid wealth-transfer tax issues after death, another excellent option is to use HECMs to assist with the transfer and create immediate income. This is a particularly good choice for Americans whose investment assets have been hit hard in recent years due to stock market turmoil; add real estate devaluation to the equation and the challenge exacerbates even further.

The very funds that retirees believed would support them during their golden years have dwindled, leaving many to wonder where in the world the additional income will come from. We have seen a lot of people losing their homes to foreclosure. Those people are now living in rentals. In fact, the demand for rentals has increased dramatically while the demand for home purchases has decreased.

One retired financial planner decided to use these market "negatives" to his advantage. Peter Thompson understood that the equity in his $895,000 home (which he owned free and clear) was an untapped asset. That money was sitting there, doing absolutely nothing for him. In fact, the home's value had dropped from $1.3 million over the last two years, making it an underperforming asset at best.

Peter is a shrewd investor but the market had been tough on him. His investment income was down, but the last thing he wanted to do was start withdrawing large amounts of principal from his retirement accounts to cover his monthly expenses. Peter also understood that the home rental market in the Northern California town where he lived was very tight, and that landlords were commanding historically high rents.

The high rent coupled with the strong buyers' market and low return on his investment portfolio lit up a light bulb above Peter's head. Armed with financial planning knowledge that he'd accumulated over the last few decades, Peter saw the opportunity to convert that home equity into cash using a HECM. Because of the hot rental market, he could then use the liquidated funds to purchase rental properties and create instant cash flow.

Peter's first idea was to buy a single rental using the cash from the proceeds from a HECM loan on his primary residence. Working closely with his Realtor, Peter quickly found four investment properties that met his needs perfectly and that would improve his cash flow more effectively than just one property. Peter bought all four of them and began generating over $4,600 per month in positive net cash flow.

Peter used proceeds from the HECM loan on his personal residence as the down payments on the four rentals. Because interest rates were so low he was able to put down just 25 percent on each property ($193,000 total across all four properties) and then he used traditional, 30-year, fixed-rate mortgage financing to fund the remaining purchase. Peter can now let his retirement accounts "come back," while he enjoys his newly found income that costs him nothing out of pocket and no monthly payments. Thanks to his HECM professional and realtor, Peter and his family are in a much better financial position regardless of their location in a geographic market that's expected to recover very slowly over the coming years.

Let's Do the Math

Peter's principal, interest, taxes, and insurance (PITI) payments on each property, are about $941 and he was able to rent out each property for approximately $2,100 per month. That puts his positive net cash flow for each home at about $1,158. Peter will continue to receive that monthly, which multiplied over four properties, puts his net income from the HECM and 4-property purchase at about $4,632 per month.

But Peter's story doesn't end there. There were also estate tax issues to address. Peter's challenge was to figure out the best way to leave those properties to his son. For estate planning purposes, Peter added his son onto the title for each property. Upon Peter's passing, his son will receive those homes without having to deal with estate planning or probate issues.

Peter's other option would have been an FLP, which would have also worked well in this situation. It would have allowed him to put each home in the partnership and divide the shares among family members. Instead, Peter and his son signed an agreement to go into partnership on the properties. Because

Peter put the deal together, he and his son agreed that he will receive the income on these properties.

The rest of Peter's estate was set up in a trust that will also transfer seamlessly to his son upon his passing. In other words, Peter has dotted all the i's and crossed the t's on his estate plan and doesn't have to worry about his estate being held up in probate or generating huge tax bills when he passes on.

The most amazing aspect of this story is the fact that Peter created the cash flow and bulletproof estate planning strategy without using one red cent. He took no money out of his pocket. He took equity from a HECM on his personal residence and pays no monthly payment on the cash that he used for down payments on four rental properties.

Peter has access to additional cash from the HECM that he can use to buy more rental properties and generate even more income. In fact, he likely has enough money to purchase at least another three to five additional properties, potentially doubling his net rental income from $4,635 to $8,000, $9,000 or possibly $10,000 per month. And to think that the money all came from a HECM that's generating no additional monthly payments.

The money Peter is using for the down payments on his rental properties is virtually payment-free and tax-free. He's putting that money into homes and generating a massive amount of cash flow. It's a strategy that works very well in today's market and will likely prevail over the next few years. Plus, he's going to be able to transfer wealth to his son without worrying about high federal and state estate taxes, probate, and other challenges that come up when someone passes on without a solid estate plan in place. Who can argue with the benefits that Peter and his family are receiving as result of this very simple financial move?

Here's how Peter used a HECM to generate retirement income and create an effective estate plan without having to withdraw on his account principal balances:

He purchased four investment properties at an average price of:	$193,000
Down payment for each property:	$48,000
Down payment percentage:	25%
Rented each home for:	$2,100
Monthly mortgage payment with taxes and insurance:	$941.05
Net income on average (per home, per month):	$1,158.94
Total net income for all four properties:	$4,635.75
Total out of pocket expenses for Peter:	0
Monthly cash flow generated by the four properties:	**$4,635.75**
Potential to increase net income to $8,000, $9,000, or $10,000	

In the next chapter we'll look at how senior homeowners can leverage the equity in their homes to avoid overburdening their adult children and to secure expensive purchases like long-term care, without generating any additional monthly payments.

Tane's Take on It

Peter can relieve any potential future tax burden from rental income or other taxable events like IRA distributions, capital gains, and so forth by paying the interest on the HECM. He can pay all the interest off by refinancing his entire HECM with a new HECM or by paying the interest with cash on hand. The interest is tax deductible once he "pays" the interest.

Information is power! I recently spoke to a financial advisor whose client had purchased three properties in Texas. He offered a bid of $60,000 each for the properties, which were appraised at the height of the real estate boom for $350,000!

He won the bid and paid cash for the three homes, which he immediately turned into rental income. The financial advisor will be sure to tell his client to consider a HECM for his next real estate play so he can leave his liquid assets invested and buy more property. The amazing thing is his client lives in Washington and the properties are in Texas – now that's thinking outside the box!

Be sure to check with your financial advisor, realtor and estate planning attorney for advice regarding your personal situation.

Four Things to Remember from Chapter Eleven

1. Estate taxes can take a big bite out of an individual's estate once that person has passed on

2. Family limited partnerships (FLPs) centralize family-held investments and/or businesses

3. A HECM is a great way to free up funding to pay for relevant, profit-producing investments in today's market

4. The money generated by a HECM to cover down payments and expenses on rental properties is virtually payment-free and tax-free

How to Avoid Burdening Your Children as You Age and Be Confident You Can Age In Place

The fact that people are living longer is a wonderful thing, but it can also be a mixed blessing for their children. According to the American Medical Association, if a man lives to the age of 65, then he has a 50 percent chance of living to the ripe old age of 91.

As that man ages he'll need more assistance and support. Doing simple things becomes harder and harder as the years go on. In fact, Medicare and Medicaid estimate that roughly 60 percent of individuals who live past 65 will require long-term care at home, adult day care, or the support of an assisted living facility. These individuals aren't necessarily "sick" in the traditional sense, but they do have trouble performing basic tasks like bathing, dressing, and eating.

Sixty percent of people over 65 will need some type of long-term care, so the odds are against you if you think you'll escape this need and expense. As medical advances continue to keep us all alive longer, the need for long-term care will also increase. Compounding the problem are the costs associated with both in-home and out-of-home elderly care. To give you an idea:

Fees for in-home care in 2011 were $48,048 per year

Assisted living facilities charge about $42,000

The median price for a private room in a nursing home is $91,250 annually

These costs are pretty steep and can put a pretty big dent in anyone's retirement reserves and fast. You can use traditional long-term care insurance policies (where you pay an annual premium to cover your nursing care, should something happen down the road) for a premium of about $2,500 to $5,000 annually, depending on your age and gender. As these policies continue to gain in popularity – and as insurance companies pay out on more and more of them – their costs are on the rise. Insurance companies are starting to get out of the long-term insurance game entirely; the risk is becoming too great for them to remain profitable.

Shelling out that much money annually for a policy that may never get used is a tough pill to swallow for some people. Sustaining such a devastating financial blow on an annual basis would be unthinkable, so they choose to ignore the issue until it becomes a "real" problem. This is the wrong approach. After all, you insure your vehicle, home, life, and other important assets – why not insure your well being too?

The questions become: 1) How do you pay for long-term care insurance, and 2) If you don't need it will it be just a big waste of money? For most people, a future health issue and/or long-term care need is impossible to predict. Ignore the issue and your children will be stuck trying to figure out how to care for you. We're seeing this unfurl right now in our society, where the "sandwich generation" (aged 40-50) is paying for their children's college expenses, managing their own lives, prepping for retirement, and taking care of their aging parents all at once. As I mentioned back in the introduction I am in the middle of the sandwich.

According to Medicare and Medicaid, the proposition of adult children providing care and assistance to a parent has more than tripled over the last 15 years, with more than 25 percent of adult children providing long-term care for their parents.

The good news is that there are some alternatives for individuals who don't want to add to that statistic. Maybe you have idle cash stored in a low-interest-bearing account such as a CD, savings account, or an old life insurance policy. You can tap into these reserves to cover your long-term care. Unfortunately, many of today's retirees and pre-retirees don't have much of these assets just lying around.

A better alternative may be to use the proceeds from a HECM to buy a life insurance policy with a long-term care rider. This allows you to combine the best features of life insurance and care into a single insurance product. Packaged as a "universal life contract," the coverage requires a single premium and funds a long-term care rider to pay out the long-term care benefits as needed. The policy also provides cash advances against your death benefit, while you are alive, to use for long-term care.

Once the premium is inside the universal life insurance policy, the account value earns an interest rate (typically at least 4 percent guaranteed) on a tax-deferred basis and accumulates a cash reserve that can be used tax-free to cover nursing or home-care costs. Any money that is not spent on nursing care benefits will be distributed to your heirs as an income tax-free death benefit under Internal Revenue Code Section 101(a)(1).

If you need nursing care, or if you can't perform your daily activities, this type of long-term care rider will cover the bases for you. Unlike traditional life insurance, these riders allow you to collect the benefits of the policy while you are still alive. In-home care is also covered by the policy. So if your life insurance policy has a face value of $200,000, then your monthly payout available for care in a nursing home would be around $4,000 (this number may vary according to your policy).

Taking out a long-term policy typically requires a lump-sum deposit (rather than the traditional monthly or systematic premium payments). To cover this expense you'll want to uncover those "lazy assets" that are earning zero return…such as your home equity. You can take those assets – or any other fixed-income investments – and use them to buy a long-term care insurance contract. If you use a HECM you won't have to make any additional monthly payments.

The cost of the policy is subtracted from the amount that will be paid to your heirs. Once you put this money into a one-time, single premium inside the life policy, it typically earns 4 percent on a tax-deferred basis and builds up cash reserves that can be used to cover nursing home or long-term care costs.

Any premium payments for the life insurance can be accessed tax free by direct withdraw or through a policy loan. Policy loans are typically set up to charge interest but the rate is the same rate of return earned inside the investment so the net charge is 0 percent interest. Not all policies have this feature so be sure to check with your insurance agent. Additionally, be sure to determine if you should fund the policy over time versus a lump sum single premium payment. If you purchase the policy with a single premium and would like to access any future gains they may be taxed. A single premium policy will trigger a modified endowment contract and could be subject to tax. To avoid the modified endowment contract you can purchase the policy over time keeping the gains tax free.

Let's Do the Math

After reviewing his long-term care options, 65-year-old John Williams of Denver decided to take the cash proceeds from his HECM and use it to add long-term care to his life insurance policy. Working with a HECM specialist and insurance agent, John was able to tap the "lazy" equity in his home and put it to good use, and all without incurring any additional monthly payments.

A non-smoker, John invested $150,000 as a single premium for the plan, which will provide $198,000 in tax-free death benefits payable to his beneficiaries upon his death. John will also receive a $594,222 income tax free benefit for long-term care. So if he needs that $91,000 in annual nursing home care he'll have access to $594,000 to cover that expense. He'll receive a maximum monthly sum of $8,253 for six years.

If John makes no withdrawals for long-term care, he'll have a guaranteed return on his initial premium. In many cases the residual death benefit is paid to the beneficiaries even if the long-term care is used by the insured. In this case, however, the $150,000 in cash that John put into his policy is guaranteed by an AAA-rated insurance company.

This new type of life policy helps you to avoid the frustration of paying premiums for a long-term care policy that might never be used. It can also work as an effective estate- planning tool that allows folks like John to remove the premium from their taxable estate or to have the policy owned by his adult children, thus also allowing the death benefit to be removed from his estate.

There are several other ways that individuals can use HECMs to fund their long-term care and take the burden off their adult children. For example, when 67-year-old Susan Daniels of Chicago wanted to leave $500,000 tax-free to her children, she used the $380,000 from a HECM to buy a single-premium life insurance policy with a long-term care rider. Susan bought the policy with a $378,640 lump sum payment and in return will receive long-term care benefits of up to $1.5 million dollars. That equates to $20,833 per month in benefits (for six years) for Susan. If she uses less than that on a monthly basis, then the benefits will last even longer.

Keep in mind $378,640 is a lot of money, but that is idle equity which wasn't doing Susan any good. She didn't incur any new monthly payments by taking out a HECM and she has peace of mind, knowing that her children will not be burdened by her should she need additional care in her later years. If Susan has an emergency and needs to access cash quickly the money is liquid inside the life insurance. However, if all the money was locked up in home equity she may have a difficult time accessing it.

Here are the calculations for John and Susan:

John Williams	
Age	65
Value of his home	$750,000
HECM	$150,000
Premium investment	$150,000

Tax-free death benefit	$594,222
Maximum monthly long-term payout	$8,253
For a period of	6 years
Guaranteed premium	$150,000
Susan Daniels	
Age	67
Value of her home	$500,000
HECM	$380,000
Tax-free death benefit	$500,000
Policy cost	$378,640
Long-term care payout	$1.5 million total
	$20,833 monthly
For a period of	Six years

Tane's Take on It

Anyone aged 65 or over who *isn't* considering their long-term care needs is taking on an unnecessary risk. Homeowners who are sitting on their home equity instead of using it to unburden their adult children are missing out on a fantastic opportunity to create a less stressful and more comfortable future for themselves and for their adult children.

Long-term care policies may sound expensive but they're actually quite affordable, particularly when they are funded through HECMs and coupled with life insurance policies. That money grows at a minimum rate of 4 percent annually and is guaranteed if the need for long-term care doesn't arise. This is a much more flexible option than the standalone long-term care policy.

With medical advancements moving at the speed of light, the odds of even longer life expectancies are right around the corner. Isn't it time to think about the future and unburden your children with a simple financial move?

Another way to fund the policy is by making annual payments for the first few years. The payment structure can reduce the overall interest accumulation on the HECM. Consult your HECM consultant and financial advisor to determine the best structure for your specific situation.

Four Things to Remember from Chapter 12

1. According to the American Medical Association, if a man lives to the age of 65, then he has a 50 percent chance of living to 91.

2. Medicare and Medicaid estimate that roughly 60 percent of individuals who live past 65 will require long-term care at home, adult day care, or the support of an assisted living facility.

3. You can use the proceeds from a HECM to buy a life insurance policy with a long-term care rider.

4. A life insurance policy with a rider allows you to combine the best features of life insurance and care into a single insurance product.

CHAPTER 13:

Use a HECM to Create
Tax-Free Income and Leave $200,000
Tax-Free to Your Children

If you're trying to decide whether to take out a HECM or leave your home for your children to inherit, I have a simple answer to your dilemma: you can use a HECM to create tax-free income for yourself *and* to leave an inheritance for your children. This is a particularly important option for women who want to leave money for their children and for men who want to make sure their spouses are taken care of in case they pass away first. A HECM can help homeowners attain both goals.

Now most retirees have their wealth tied up in home equity. By tapping into that equity with a HECM, those retirees can literally have their cake and eat it too. According to financial advisor John Peters from Orange, Calif., using a HECM to increase retirement income and leave a legacy to your heirs is a very good option for homeowners. He illustrates his points through the real-life stories of Mr. and Mrs. Madson, aged 70 and 68, respectively. In very good health, the couple was living on a pension that was more than enough to cover their living expenses. But like many aging Americans, the Madsons watched their medical expenses climb significantly over the last few years. Their property taxes also rose and these extra costs began to take up more and more of their retirement income.

But before the Madsons retired, they paid off their home, which is now valued at $300,000. Peters suggested a HECM, but the Madsons were reluctant based on the fact that leaving a financial legacy (not necessarily the home itself) to their children was important to them. After some discussion, they decided that they'd like to leave $100,000 to each child for a total of $200,000. Using a HECM, they would be able to achieve that goal and also increase their monthly income by about $700.

According to Peters, the Madsons used a HECM to generate a guaranteed income stream of $1,000 per month for the rest of their lives as long as they resided in their home. From that $1,000, they used $302.14 to purchase a second-to-die guaranteed universal life insurance contract that would pay an income-tax-free death benefit of $200,000 upon the death of the second spouse. Each child was listed as a beneficiary at 50 percent each (or $100,000 for each child). The guaranteed death benefit would stay in place until the Madsons reached 110 years of age, making it unlikely that they would outlive the insurance contract and leaving them with an additional $697.86 every month to cover those rising medical and property tax costs.

By staying in their home and taking out the second-to-die universal life insurance policy, the Madsons will now be able to live more comfortably and leave a financial legacy for their children. As you can see, this worked out much better than selling the $300,000 home, downsizing to free up extra cash, and then making unpredictable investments in different types of accounts.

Tane's Take on It

The Madsons had another option at their avail. They could have sold their home for $300,000 and then used a HECM for purchase to buy a $200,000 property for $98,000. That would have left the couple $202,000 to use for a structured income plan. The cash flow created by this strategy would be guaranteed at 5.77 percent and would generate $971.28 per month for the Madsons. If they use the $302.14 of the $971.28 for the life insurance policy, they would still have $669.14 left for lifestyle and living expenses. The $302.14 will be used to purchase the universal life insurance with a second-to-die rider and would leave their children a $223,556 tax-free inheritance.

Four Things to Remember from Chapter 13

1. Most retirees have their wealth tied up in home equity.

2. Using a HECM to increase retirement income and leave a legacy to heirs is a very good option for homeowners.

3. You can use a HECM to create tax-free income for yourself and to leave an inheritance for your children.

4. A HECM is a good option for women who want to leave money for their children and for men who want to make sure their spouses are taken care of in case they pass away first.

CHAPTER 14:

Create a Legacy and Leave $1 Million or More to Your Favorite Charity

If you are anything like me, you want to be remembered for something more than just putting in 20-40 years working for a company. The typical obituary these days focuses on the deceased's occupation, birthplace, survivors, and place of worship. I'd like my obituary to go beyond that and center on how I've left a legacy of giving that will literally go on perpetually.

If it sounds like a lofty goal, you'll definitely want to read this chapter and take away some of the sage advice you'll find in the next few pages of this book.

Let's start by looking at the obstacles that stand in the way of establishing and leaving such legacies. In many cases, while the intentions of leaving preserved wealth in perpetuity for charitable organizations sounds like a terrific move, we usually lack the wealth to do this. We aren't sitting on multimillion-dollar bank accounts like the Bill Gates and Warren Buffetts of the world, nor do we know how to go about accumulating such assets. We read a lot about other folks who set up foundations and charities (namely, celebrities and very successful businesspeople), but becoming one of them is a pipedream for most of us.

Even moderately well-off individuals don't know how to tackle the problem. They have millions stashed in retirement accounts and likely own one or more homes that are worth upwards of $1 million. They have sizable net worths, but not enough to be giving away $1-$2 million to outside sources, and a drive to leave sizable estates behind for their children.

Doing more than that is reserved for "other people" of greater means. Or is it? Millions of Americans make donations of cash and property to the charities of their choice each year. While these donations can provide valuable tax deductions, many donors are left wishing they could do more for the charities that they love and support.

Life insurance policies can help fill that gap and serve as an effective way to leverage charitable support. Couple those policies with a HECM – a cash reserve that generates no additional monthly payments and effectively uses lazy, underperforming assets – and you get a magical combination that can make pretty much anyone feel like Bill Gates in their own right.

This chapter of this book is particularly poignant because we are all givers at heart. We are put on this earth to give our time, talent, and treasure. Here are some statistics from Giving USA 2011, the Annual Report on Philanthropy, published by the AAFRC Trust for Philanthropy:

— Total giving to charitable organizations was $290.89 billion in 2010 (about 2% of GDP). This is an increase of 3.8% from 2009 when giving was $280.3 billion.

— As in previous years, the majority of that giving came from individuals. Specifically, individuals gave $211.77 billion (73%) representing a 2.7% increase over 2009.

— Giving by bequest was $22.83 billion (up 18.8%), foundations gave $41 billion (down 0.2%), and corporations donated $15.29 billion (up 10.6%).

— 35% of all donations, or $100.63 billion, went to religious organizations (up only 0.8%). Much of these contributions can be attributed to people giving to their local place of worship. The next largest sector was education with $41.67 billion (up 5.2%).

— Donations were also up to foundations (1.9%), health charities (1.3%), public benefit charities (6.2%), arts, culture, and humanities charities (5.7%). International charities saw the biggest growth in giving (15.3%), in part, because of the earthquake in Haiti (January 2010).

— Giving to several categories of charities was virtually flat in 2010 including donations to human services, environmental, and animal charities.

— Revised Giving USA data shows that total giving has grown in current dollars in every year since 1954 except for 1987, 2008 and 2009.

I want to show you how you can achieve part of that goal of leveraging your own treasure by giving back to the charities that are closet to your hearts in perpetuity. The death benefit associated with your life insurance policy can supply charities with the critical resources that they need to meet their goals.

Known as "charitable giving riders," these addendums can be attached to policies with face values of over $1 million. They pay out an additional 1-2% of the policy's face value to a qualified charity of the policyholder's choice, although sometimes there are limitations placed on the maximum allowable gift amount. The riders cost nothing and typically don't increase the premium, reduce the cash value, or the death benefit of the policy. These riders effectively eliminate the need to create, pay for, and administrate separate gift trusts until the death of the insured.

A life insurance policy gives a tremendous amount of leverage and the death benefit usually exceeds the total premiums paid. In fact, individuals can pass two or three times the value of their homes onto charity. That means a $1 million home would translate into $2-$3 million for the target charity or charities. Those death benefits are delivered when the policy matures. If kept in force, the policy proceeds are paid upon the insured's death regardless of how many premiums have been paid. The policy owner has the right to change the timing and the amount of payments, as well as the amount of the death benefit and the named beneficiary.

A life insurance policy has the potential to make a charitable gift much larger than the premiums that were ever paid into it. It can effectively produce gifting "leverage" because the death benefits it produces usually exceed the premiums paid in. As a result, a policy has the potential to increase your charitable legacy. Whether any leverage is produced depends on the size of the policy death benefit, the health and life expectancy of the insured, and the number of premiums paid.

Let's Do the Math

Martha McPherson is just one of millions of Americans who want to leave a legacy behind. She wanted to transfer $1 million to her church upon her death. Martha knew that money would go a long way in helping to support the local soup kitchen, youth program, and other church-related initiatives.

A 65-year-old non-smoker and in good health, Martha was able to purchase a $1 million policy for herself with a single premium payment of $380,000. She accessed her equity and took out a HECM. She purchased the life insurance policy without creating any additional monthly payments for herself.

Martha created $1 million out of $380,000 and still retained $336,000 in equity in her home. All Martha had to do was name her church as the beneficiary to have the $1 million transferred to the organization upon her death – no questions asked.

The multiplier effect and the fact that she had no out-of-pocket expenses were both extremely attractive for Martha. Her home equity was just sitting there, creating no value for anyone. Suddenly just a portion of it was nearly tripled and willed to her cherished nonprofit organization. It was a dream come true for Martha.

The benefits don't end there. Martha is also earning a guaranteed, fixed return of 4 percent inside of her life insurance contract; that money helps offset the interest that's accruing (with no payments) on her HECM. When Martha passes away, her home will be sold and the leftover equity will be passed onto her heirs as part of her estate. Finally, she can access money from her life insurance policy whenever needed.

Here are the calculations for Martha McPherson:

Martha's age	65
Home value	$735,000
Single premium life insurance cost	$380,000
HECM proceeds	$386,835
Life insurance policy value	$1,000,000

Tane's Take on It

We all have an amazing opportunity to leave a legacy behind that goes beyond our job titles, years of service, and birthplace. You can do this by leveraging the untapped equity in your home through a HECM. You'll pay no additional monthly fees and you'll be able to use the equity – which was just sitting there anyway – to buy a single-premium life insurance policy at a lump sum. You name the beneficiaries (your children, a charity, or both) and then leverage that $200,000 to $500,000 via a HECM and move that over to a life insurance policy.

This move will give you two to three times the value of what you put into it. It's an amazing tool that will ensure that your legacy lives long into perpetuity, and that your favorite charity is well supported long after you are gone. It's a dream that's no longer reserved for the multimillionaires of the world – it's within your grasp!

Four Things to Remember from Chapter 14

1. We are all givers at heart and we all want to leave behind more than just a basic obituary.

2. You don't have to be Bill Gates to establish a substantial financial resource for your favorite charity.

3. You can leverage the untapped equity in your home through a HECM and then use that cash to purchase a single-premium life insurance policy.

4. Homeowners can effectively leverage their life insurance policies to give out two to three times the amount of their investment to their charities of choice.

CHAPTER 15:

Ready, Set, Go!

HECMs are excellent financial, estate, and tax planning tools for a diverse cross section of senior homeowners. They are not limited to those that are in a dire need of cash, as you've read throughout this book, nor are they the domain of the super rich who want to protect their wealth.

Universal in nature, HECMs are a valuable tool for home-owners who would otherwise underutilize non-performing assets without ever realizing the leveraging capabilities of that wealth.

With the first of the nation's 78 million Baby Boomers turning 68 next year, the opportunity to help these folks tap into their hidden wealth and transform it into investment income (to buy more real estate); liquid cash (to help loved ones out of foreclosure); long-term insurance premiums; and several other "performing" options are virtually limitless.

Realtors, insurance agents, financial advisors and HECM specialists, are just a few of the professionals who will be called upon to help explain the process, walk consumers through their options, and ultimately help clients makes the best possible choices regarding their HECMs.

With this book as your guide, you'll be well equipped to answer the call and/or even make a few good choices regarding your own home equity.

Here are your next action steps:

If you received this book from a real estate agent, insurance agent, financial advisor, or HECM professional I encourage you to meet with them to "run your numbers" and see how the power of using the strategies can play out in your own life. If you don't have a professional you can contact, please visit our website doubleyourretirementdollars.com/referral for a qualified one in your area.

If this book has impacted you please don't keep it a secret. You can purchase additional copies to give to your friends and advisors. Please visit Amazon.com to purchase additional copies. Discounted bulk orders may be purchased at doubleyourretirementdollars.com

For additional information and the latest strategies and tools please visit **doubleyourretirementdollars.com**

Additional Resources

To obtain a copy of the actual letter that the Department of Housing and Urban Development issued regarding the Home Equity Conversion Mortgage for Purchase Program visit http://www.hud.gov and enter in the search area the following: **"MORTGAGEE LETTER 2008-33"**. To obtain the most updated revised version enter the following in the search section: **MORTGAGEE LETTER 2009-11"**

Purchase Calculation Form

Wondering how to figure out the best calculation for a HECM purchase? Download the latest version of the form by visiting: **doubleyourretirementdollars.com/purchaseform.**

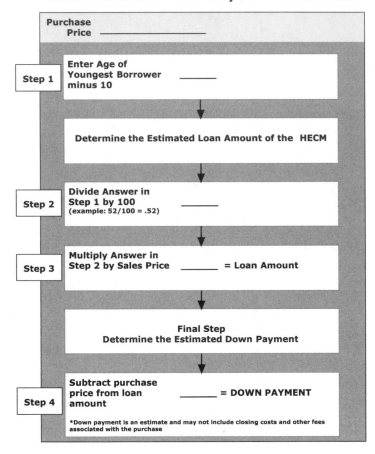

Name: _____   Date: _____

HECM Purchase Down Payment Determiner

Purchase Price _____

Step 1
Enter Age of
Youngest Borrower _____
minus 10

Determine the Estimated Loan Amount of the HECM

Step 2
Divide Answer in
Step 1 by 100 _____
(example: 52/100 = .52)

Step 3
Multiply Answer in
Step 2 by Sales Price _____ = Loan Amount

Final Step
Determine the Estimated Down Payment

Step 4
Subtract purchase
price from loan _____ = DOWN PAYMENT
amount

*Down payment is an estimate and may not include closing costs and other fees associated with the purchase

Steps of a HECM Purchase Transaction

1. Use the HECM Purchase Down Payment Determiner Form to calculate your down payment on a new purchase

2. If you have a home to sell determine how much equity you have in the home and the net proceeds you will

receive by discussing your home value with a real estate agent. If you don't have a home to sell and you currently rent you will need to determine and prove the source of the down payment.

3. Sign your final agreement to sell your home with a real estate agent that knows the process of a HECM purchase.

4. Look for a home that you wish to purchase while your home is on the market for sale.

5. Complete HECM counseling by a HUD approved HECM counselor.

6. Once your home is sold or is under contract with a buyer, make an offer on the new home with a qualification letter provided by a HECM professional that is familiar with the HECM purchase program. At this time you would have completed a HECM application. Please note: If the home is new construction you cannot complete a HECM application until there is a certificate of occupancy provided by the local building authority. This can cause delays in closing and all parties must be aware of this specific restriction.

7. Sign you final closing papers and the lender will fund the loan. Once the loan is funded and recorded the new home is yours!

Standard HECM Calculation Form

Wondering how to figure out the best calculation for a standard HECM? Download the latest version of the form by visiting: **doubleyourretirementdollars.com/standardform**

Name: Date:

HECM Estimated Loan Proceeds Determiner

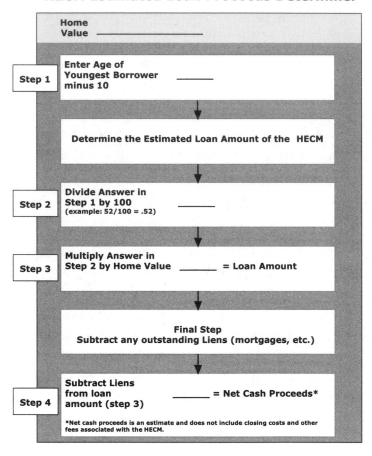

Home Value _____

Step 1 — Enter Age of Youngest Borrower minus 10 _____

Determine the Estimated Loan Amount of the HECM

Step 2 — Divide Answer in Step 1 by 100
(example: 52/100 = .52) _____

Step 3 — Multiply Answer in Step 2 by Home Value _____ = Loan Amount

Final Step
Subtract any outstanding Liens (mortgages, etc.)

Step 4 — Subtract Liens from loan amount (step 3) _____ = Net Cash Proceeds*

*Net cash proceeds is an estimate and does not include closing costs and other fees associated with the HECM.

HECM Terms

— **Appraisal:** As with any mortgage, an appraisal is required. An appraisal is the process of inspecting a home's condition and assessing the market value of the home. Typically the borrowers pay for the appraisal as part of their closing costs upfront.

— **Cash (Lump Sum Cash Advance):** HECM borrowers can receive their HECM payout in cash – a single lump sum. HECM payouts can be customized with a mix of different payout options.

— **Closing Costs:** Closing costs on a HECM are the costs a borrower must pay to secure a HECM. HECM closing costs are sometimes criticized for being too high, but they can actually be paid with the HECM itself, so there are usually few out of pocket expenses. These fees may include an origination fee, title insurance appraisal, closing fee, pest and other inspections, a credit report, and more.

— **Counselor / HECM Counselor:** The federal government mandates that all HECM borrowers meet with a HUD approved counselor before completing a HECM application. The counselor is approved by HUD and explains the advantages, disadvantages, and alternatives to a HECM.

— **The Department of Housing and Urban Development (HUD):** HUD defines itself as the Nation's Housing Agency. It is a federal department committed to increasing homeownership. HUD is the creator of the Home Equity Conversion Mortgage, HECM.

— **Federally Insured:** The HECM product is federally insured. The federal government guarantees payment on any loan default.

— **Fully Indexed Rate:** The Fully Indexed Rate is the interest rate that you pay on a HECM that carries an adjustable rate. The interest rate charged is calculated by adding the index rate plus the margin. The rate will also carry a maximum rate that can be calculated.

— **HECM Standard:** The HECM Standard is the original program offered by HUD and offers the largest amount of money of any HECM program, but carries a higher fee structure.

— **Home Equity:** Your home equity is the value of your home minus any balance on your mortgage. When closing a HECM any mortgage liens on the home must be paid off before receiving additional proceeds from the HECM.

— **Home Equity Conversion Mortgage (HECM):** The HECM is the most popular type of HECM and is the only HECM insured by HUD.

— **HUD:** See The Department of Housing and Urban Development.

— **Interest Rate Caps:** Interest Rate Caps are a preset maximum interest rate that may be charged over the life of the loan. Interest rate caps determine the maximum allowable rate on an adjustable rate HECM. The Fully Indexed Rate of the HECM loan cannot exceed the Interest Rate Cap.

— **Lending Limits:** A lending limit is the maximum HECM loan amount that any home would qualify for based on its geographic location. The county determines HECM lending limits.

— **Home Value Limits:** The maximum home value that can be considered in determining the amount of loan (or line of credit) available. Since 2009 it has been set at $625,500. Although prior to this time the value limit was $417,000. The home can be valued more than the limit and still qualify, but loan will be limited based on the maximum value of $625,500.

— **Lien:** A lien is a legal claim against property that acts as security against payment of debts.

— **Line of Credit:** A popular payout method for a HECM is a line of credit. The entire HECM loan amount is available to you in a line of credit and accessible as needed.

— **Loan Amount:** Loan amount is the term that refers to the actual amount you are eligible to borrow with a HECM. The loan amount is determined by the lending limit, home value, age, and interest rates.

— **Margin:** The margin and the index are the two components that, when combined, comprise the final interest rate at which the HECM accrues interest.

— **Modified Tenure:** This is a HECM payout option that combines a line of credit with monthly payments, similar to an annuity.

— **Mortgage Insurance:** The HECM requires mortgage

insurance. The premium is paid up front and an annual premium of ½ a percent of the loan balance. This is paid to the FHA by the borrower but generally through the loan proceeds. The insurance protects you and your heirs in case the loan balance exceeds the value. If this "upside down" situation happens the insurance will pay for any shortfall. You are not personally responsible because of the mortgage insurance protection.

— **Origination Fee:** HECMs can carry an origination fee charged by the lender for processing the application and making the loan. Borrowers are able to finance the entire amount of the origination fee as part of the mortgage.

— **Payout Options:** The money from a HECM can come to you in one of three different payout options:
1. Lump sum of cash
2. Monthly amount
3. Line of Credit where interest on the loan is only charged on the money used. The line of credit also grows over time by a fixed percent, known as the credit line growth rate.

— **Primary Residence:** A HECM can only be taken on a primary residence. A primary residence is defined as the property you occupy for more than 50% of the year.

— **Qualifications:** Qualifying for a HECM means a minimum age of 62 years old and owning a home with enough equity (generally 50% or more). There are no income, health, or credit qualifications.

— **Tenure Option:** Tenure option refers to a payout option for your loan that provides equal monthly payments as long as it remains the primary home.

— **Total Annual Loan Cost (TALC):** The TALC is the average combined annual costs of the HECM loan. This is a useful figure to use when comparing different loans. Visit: **doubleyourretirementdollars.com/shopping** to watch a video on "How to Shop for A HECM"

Top Ten
Frequently Asked Questions
Regarding a HECM

1. What is a HECM?

A HECM is a special type of home loan that lets you convert a portion of the equity in your home into cash. The equity that you built up over years of making mortgage payments can be paid to you. However, unlike a traditional home equity loan or second mortgage, HECM borrowers do not have to repay the HECM loan until the borrowers no longer use the home as their principal residence. You can also use a HECM to purchase a primary residence if you are able to use cash on hand to pay the difference between the HECM proceeds and the sales price plus closing costs for the property you are purchasing.

2. Can I qualify for FHA's HECM?

To be eligible for a FHA HECM, the FHA requires that you be a homeowner 62 years of age or older, own your home outright, or have a low mortgage balance that can be paid off at closing with proceeds from the reverse loan, and you must live in the home. You are also required to receive consumer information free or at very low cost (generally between $80 and $150) from a HECM counselor prior to obtaining the loan. You can find one by phoning (800) 569-4287. When you call the number you will be able to locate a HUD approved counselor to obtain your required HECM counseling.

3. Can I apply for a HECM even if I did not buy my present house with FHA mortgage insurance?

Yes. You may apply for a HECM regardless of whether or not you purchased your home with an FHA-insured mortgage.

4. What types of homes are eligible?

To be eligible for the FHA HECM, your home must be a single family home or a 2-4 unit home with one unit occupied by the borrower. HUD-approved condominiums and manufactured homes that meet FHA requirements are also eligible.

5. What are the differences between a HECM and a home equity loan?

With a second mortgage, or a home equity line of credit, borrowers must have adequate income to qualify for the loan, and they make monthly payments on the principal and interest. A HECM is different, because it pays you – there are no monthly principal and interest payments. With a HECM, you are required to pay real estate taxes, utilities, and hazard and flood insurance premiums.

6. Will we have an estate that we can leave to heirs?

When the home is sold or no longer used as a primary residence, the cash, interest, and other HECM finance charges must be repaid. All proceeds beyond the amount owed belong to your spouse or estate. This means any remaining equity can be transferred to heirs. No debt is passed along to the estate or heirs.

7. How much money can I get from my home?

The amount you may borrow will depend on:

- Age of the youngest borrower
- Current interest rate
- Lesser of appraised value or the HECM FHA value limit of $625,500
- Initial Mortgage Insurance Premium via the HECM Standard.

You can borrow more with the HECM Standard option. In addition, the more valuable your home is, the older you are, and the lower the interest rate, the more you can borrow. If there is more than one borrower, the age of the youngest borrower is used to determine the amount you can borrow. For an estimate of HECM cash benefits, select the online calculator by visiting doubleyourretirementdollars.com/calculator

8. How do I find a HECM lender?

The best way to find a HECM lender is by getting a competent referral from a professional whom you trust. You may also visit doubleyourretirementdollars.com/referral to find a professional in your area.

9. **How do I receive my payments?**

You can select from five payment plans:

Tenure- Equal monthly payments as long as at least one borrower lives and continues to occupy the property as a principal residence.

Term- Equal monthly payments for a fixed period of months selected.

Line of Credit- Unscheduled payments or in installments, at times and in an amount of your choosing until the line of credit is exhausted.

Modified Tenure- Combination of line of credit and scheduled monthly payments for as long as you remain in the home.

Modified Term- Combination of line of credit plus monthly payments for a fixed period of months selected by the borrower.

10. **What if I change my mind and no longer want the loan after I go to closing? How do I do this?**

By law, you have three calendar days to change your mind and cancel the loan. This is called a three day right of rescission. The process of canceling the loan should be explained at loan closing. Be sure to ask the lender for instructions on this process. Mortgage lenders differ in the process of canceling a loan. You should ask for the names of the appropriate people, phone numbers, fax numbers, addresses, or written instructions on whatever process the company has in place. In most cases, the right of rescission will not be applicable to HECM for purchase transactions.

Notes

_____

_____

_____

_____

_____

_____

_____

_____

_____

_____

_____

_____

_____

_____

_____

_____

_____